IF I COULD,
SO CAN YOU!

The man behind the Paul Davis
franchise phenomenon, in his own words

IF I COULD, SO CAN YOU!

The man behind the Paul Davis
franchise phenomenon, in his own words

Paul Woodall Davis

PWD
Jacksonville, Florida U.S.A.

Davis, Paul Woodall, 1927–
If I Could, So Can You! The man behind the Paul Davis franchise
phenomenon, in his own words / Paul Woodall Davis. —1ˢᵗ ed.
Issued also in PDF and ePUB format.

ISBN 978-0-9975247-0-3 (Paperback)
ISBN 978-0-9975247-1-0 (PDF)
ISBN 978-0-9975247-2-7 (ePUB)

Editor: Jacquelyn Waller-Vintar
Designer: Brent Baughman
Photographs supplied by author
Set in Garamound

DEDICATION

This book is dedicated to all those early franchise owners and Paul Davis staff members who stayed faithful as we refined Paul Davis Systems.

It took belief in the system, patience and hard work to bring it to where it is today. You should all be proud.

It is also dedicated to my wife, Brenda, and our entire family of children and grandchildren who have been and are the most important part of my life.

CONTENTS

Chapter 4

Chapter 5

Chapter 6

Chapter 7
Some People Who Have Influenced My Life 69

Chapter 8

FOREWORD

The Brady Bunch we are not, never have been and never will be!

However, in 1989 Paul and I brought together our seven diverse children, who were about as diverse as their parents. The kids ranged in age from nine to forty, and we won't discuss the age of the parents (there were already grandchildren on Paul's side).

Here we are, some twenty-six years later, more grandchildren, more sons- and daughters-in-law. Everyone is still family. No dropouts in this mixed-up group.

Paul and I met fifty years ago. As I read his memoir, it's not news or surprising to me. Even though I lived in California, we had family ties that brought us to Jacksonville frequently, so Paul and Loyce were close and our families stayed in touch.

When I was going through a sad divorce from a marriage of thirty years and not sure what to do with myself, I was thrilled that Paul called and asked if I might be interested in coming to Jacksonville to work in his growing business. Since my background was primarily in Southern Baptist work and owning a personal improvement and charm franchise, I was not sure how I would fit into the insurance restoration contracting business. But I accepted and moved to Jacksonville. Soon after, my adult sons followed. All three had finished college and were establishing their own careers.

The rest is history. Not long afterward I fell in love with and married the boss, Paul W. Davis.

The PWD Inc. family welcomed me with the same spirit of acceptance and thoughtfulness that ran through the culture and value system of the entire company.

Most people who know Paul would agree that the characteristics they experienced in the business life of Paul are the same as those in his personal life. His deep belief of treating people with acceptance, appreciation, respect and kindness spanned across his entire life. He never forgets his feelings of inferiority and has done his best to keep others from feeling that pain themselves.

Life has been and is good living with Paul Davis. Perfect, no, not at all (that's a story for another time). It is an adventure; it has been and is a beautiful love between two people who love and accept each other, because we do.

This book contains snippets of Paul Davis, his business successes and failures, and his systems approach to life, both business and personal. Everything must have a system, according to him.

The value system and culture of Paul Davis, the company, really is who Paul Davis, the person, is.

I hope his next book will be about overcoming obstacles and creating an environment that makes it possible to help people know how to love and respect others. And learn how to forgive others. He is good at that.

I trust you will enjoy reading about part of the journey as we have lived it.

Brenda Davis

PREFACE

As much as I enjoy writing, I enjoy the writings of others. I particularly appreciate well-worded pithy statements that I can relate to my own life. I've been saving sayings, quotes, fragments of my own writing, turning them into mantras and using them for inspiration, for decades. In my personal and business lives, they've come to be known as "Paul's pearls." I offer up this selection, beginning with Matthew 23:11, as a glimpse of my personal belief system.

Let he who is greatest among you, be the servant of all.

You may not be who you think you are. But you are continually becoming the product of what you think.

An objective without appropriate processes is just a dream.

Honesty and integrity are essential for a well-balanced, rewarding life.

It is far more exciting and enjoyable becoming successful than it is being successful.

The saddest state known to man is to have accomplished all his goals.

Forgiving is essential if you wish to experience a low-stress life.

Always look at the present realistically and objectively. Always look at the future through rose-colored glasses.

Always take total responsibility for who, what and where you are.

Problems are, almost without exception, the result of something you did that you should not have done, or something you did not do that you should have done.

Things almost always work out to the good of those who believe they will and very seldom for those who do not believe they will.

Believing, accepting, forgiving, caring and loving are simple acts of our God-given will. They are not hard to do; you just have to will to do them.

What you consistently think as though it were so, almost always becomes so, good or bad.

There is no higher goal than to seek to make someone's life better by your words and deeds.

It is unfair to criticize someone for failing to meet your expectations if you have never made an effort to define and help your people to understand them.

The number of people who rust out far exceeds the number who burn out.

There is a vast difference between problems, which can generally be solved, and circumstances, which require adjusting and coping but always linger until someone or something changes to relieve the situation. Recognizing the difference and reacting appropriately, eliminates a lot of stress.

Forgiveness provides far greater value to the forgiver than to the forgiven, who may never know that the forgiveness has been granted.

You are not responsible for the actions of others, but you are fully responsible for your reaction to those actions.

Never give a gift expecting a certain outcome. If the outcome is that important, find a way to give the outcome. Otherwise, the act of giving, which should produce great joy, may create hurt for the giver and probably the receiver.

INTRODUCTION

As a young child, I learned the joy of helping others from my mother. It seemed she was always taking chicken soup, fried chicken or peach cobbler to someone who was sick or had a need. Many times she had me and my brothers milking a cow, raking a yard or whatever needed doing for friends or neighbors who needed a helping hand.

I soon found out how good it felt to know that I had helped someone, just because. And doing those things, those acts of kindness, helped me to commit to doing what I could for others for the rest of my life, including whatever time I have left.

As an adult, being active in our church was an opportunity to minister to people on a regular basis, so it seemed logical to me that I needed to become a minister or a missionary. But God had other ideas for me. I fully believe that He brought me to the insurance restoration contracting business to fulfill a dream of reaching out to people on a large scale.

Throughout my early years, I was fortunate that I worked with people who shared my dream of helping others and taught me how to do that and earn a living for my family as well. It started with insurance adjusters asking me to help out with insurance-covered jobs. But it didn't take me long to realize that those hurting property owners were our real customers. When I walked into a home where the property owner had lost almost everything they had, they needed someone who would care about them enough to put them back, as closely as possible, to normal.

Standing in a charred and flooded home, I would try to put myself into the owners' shoes. From there it was a small step to adopt the Golden Rule—Do unto others as you would have them do unto you—as the official culture of Paul Davis Systems, and the 1911 Rotary motto—He profits most who serves best—as a guiding principle.

There are many, many stories from franchise owners that show how abiding by these two sayings became, through the years, as natural as doing estimates. One such experience I remember happened when a Kentucky franchise owner went out to see a kitchen fire loss. The elderly owner lived alone, and her greatest distress was a ceramic table her late husband had made her many years earlier. Even though the table was not really damaged by the fire, it was broken. Realizing her heartbreak the franchisee offered to take it with him and see what he could do, although others had told her it could not be repaired. A few days later he returned her table looking like it did before the fire. Needless to say, this lady was thrilled, which would have been enough for the franchisee, but he got to do the job as well. He became good friends with her; her trust in him was complete. When the job was finished, she asked him to write the check for payment out of her own checkbook. This is what caring and putting the customer first meant to her.

As I reflect on these past fifty years I can truthfully say there have been many of these stories and of franchise owners applying this culture to their businesses as we taught it in our training school and lived it as the franchisor. It became the very heartbeat of Paul Davis the franchisor.

I remember when Brenda became a part of the company in 1990. We appointed her as Service of Excellence Director. Her job was to be the go-to person for the franchisees as well as the employees of the home office. Her very nature is caring and she took this emphasis to a higher level.

We had an employee who retired on a Friday with a big sendoff and the following Monday found that she had inoperable cancer. With her retirement, this lovely single lady lost her insurance and had no income. We agreed that we would put her back on active duty at full pay with her returning to the office only if she improved. She passed away not long afterward. Before she passed, she shed many tears of gratitude that she could maintain some degree of independence in her last days.

Caring is action, not just words! I feel a sense of real pride and give thanks that I was able to create a business based on this philosophy. And yes I do feel joy and peace that God gave me not only the heart to care, but that there are thousands of people who have in one way or another profited from this culture.

I now spend time reflecting on and thanking God for the opportunity and wisdom to meet my needs and the needs of thousands of others as well. In my retirement at eighty-eight, I can enjoy remembering the successes of starting and growing Paul Davis, the company. I have memories of the hundreds of really good people who were part of the franchise organization; people who now enjoy their own successes. And knowing that I started something that touches the lives of so many people in many different ways is forever with me.

Sure, there are times when nostalgia causes me to wonder why I sold the company; why I thought I was ready to see my dream come to an end in my own lifetime. I can truly say that I loved it. The day-to-day working in it. I have always believed that becoming successful is far more enjoyable than being successful.

However, when I watch what FirstService Brands is doing to tremendously expand on the foundation of my dream, I can't help but feel a great sense of gratification and pride in that goal of becoming the number one franchised insurance restoration organization in the world. And that its leaders and staff are committed to continue the caring culture that came out of my need to serve others. The motto

"He profits most who serves best" (I have to add that the Rotary updated this motto in 2010, to "One profits most who serves best") continues on today.

My heart is truly fulfilled and I can honestly say I am proud to carry the name of Paul Davis.

Chapter 1
EARLY DAYS

My Youth

My life started in 1927 in a small house on a small lake about ten miles outside of Lake Wales, Florida.

I was the seventh and last child of seven boys born to my mother, Mary Susan Woodall. The first two died of crib death, each of them at nine months of age. My mother told the story of when her third son, Joe, came to that same age she lived in utter terror that she would look in the crib and find Joe dead. It did not happen. Momma had Joe and then Bob; her first husband, Joseph Daniel Jeffords, died three years after Bob's birth. She married my father, Charles C. Davis, Sr., and they had Charles, Jr., William and me, the baby of the family. My father worked for Independent Life Insurance Company as a salesman and debit collector.

When I was still a baby, we were forced to leave our little home-steaded cabin by a hurricane. My parents and siblings each took what they could and we all crowded into Daddy's Model T Ford for the drive to Lake Wales to move in with relatives.

All went well until we reached the railroad track where, for some unknown reason, the car just stopped and would not start again.

Momma carried me and each of the others took what they could carry, and we made the balance of the ten-mile walk down the rail-road tracks to a relative's house. It was a harrowing struggle in heavy darkness, unsure footing on rocks and railroad ties, with blinding lightning and roaring thunder, then utter darkness, all the while being pelted with unrelenting rain. Trees fell; limbs broke loose and flew across the railroad bed. There was no way to measure our progress, no lights to encourage us forward, and no one to call out to but each other. A crying baby and two little boys, stumbling and hoping for the best as my parents prayed for the end, whatever that would be.

They stayed the course and finally came to my aunt's house where they were met with love and grateful hearts on all sides. My mother, father and siblings' perseverance were a testimony to the strength of our family.

Shortly thereafter, Daddy was transferred to Jacksonville and then to Fernandina and then back to Jacksonville where he and Momma spent the rest of their lives.

I don't remember much about the time we lived in Fernandina except for being hit by a car as I crossed the street to a store where the owner would always give me a piece of candy. I was halfway across the street and the lady behind the wheel did not see me until it was too late to stop. From what I have been told, I was hit, then spun round and round and collapsed on the ground. My mother heard the commotion and rushed out to find her worst fear to be a fact.

She scooped me up, took me inside, placed me on the daybed in the front room and called the doctor. He came quickly. He determined I had no broken bones and instructed my mother to let me rest and he would return later in the day. (Don't be too quick to judge my mother. She was making do in a small house with all five of us crammed into four small rooms. No mother could be more caring, although she did not show a lot of outward affection.)

Each time someone would try to move me in any manner I would begin to cry and scream and did not stop until I was laid back down. After six weeks, the doctor decided that he would give it one more day and if I still could not move, he would admit me to the local hospital.

In desperation, my mother began to put her hand under my neck and massage it gently. As she continued to massage, she slowly lifted my head a few inches at a time. And over the course of the afternoon, she was finally able to raise me into her arms and begin to rock me.

Not too long after this event, Daddy was transferred back to Jacksonville and assigned to a South Jacksonville debit route. He and Momma bought an 800-square-foot house on Ryar Road, just off of Hogan Road (now Beach Boulevard) for $800, payable $8 per month, and that is where they spent the rest of their lives and raised their three remaining children.

I was, for no particular reason, plagued by a serious inferiority complex growing up—what we call today low self-esteem, which sounds a little nicer. I grew up thinking I was both dumb and ugly. No one ever told me I was, but I don't remember anyone telling me I was not either.

Being the fifth of my mother's living children and the fourth for my father and being raised through the Great Depression and World War II, my parents did all they could do to keep me safe, fed and clothed.

I won't go into a lot of detail about my childhood, but one more event is worth telling. Someone had given me a little sailboat and the closest spot for me to sail it was an abandoned dipping vat where cows were led through to clear them of ticks and dirt.

I took my little sailboat, unbeknownst to my mother, and walked up the road to the dipping vat. I commenced playing in water that had not been emptied for several years. At one point, I leaned too far out to reach my boat and ended up in the stagnant water. I couldn't swim but when I came up for air I began to scream as loudly as possible. Fortunately, a man was working nearby and came quickly enough to pull me out and save my life.

I went home crying to be received with a strong hug by a crying mother, and immediately thereafter a strong switch on my bare legs.

One of my core beliefs is that there is some good to be found in almost all life situations. That proved to be true in this case, because I never remember being bothered by ticks again.

Education

My school days got off to a rough start. I remember only two things about my early grades.

At recess, we would go outside to play. For the boys that was finding and catching flies. The object was to sneak up close and with a quick swipe of the hand catch the fly. I won't thrill you with what followed. One recess I spotted the biggest and blackest fly I had ever seen. I slowly moved into position and with a quick swipe closed the fly into my hand. I felt a very strong stinging pain and quickly opened my hand to find that bumblebees don't like to be considered flies. And my very swollen and hurting hand proved their point.

The second memory was of the first day of Grade 2 when the class was being moved to the Grade 2 day room. Everyone was moved except for me and two others. I did not understand why, but I knew I was left behind and feeling left out. I began to cry. The teacher was touched and decided to let me go to second grade.

In retrospect, that might have been the beginning of my school years of always just getting by. I was never a good student, but time has proven that the cause was not a lack of intelligence or a problem of rejection. The problem was low self-esteem: my firm belief that I was both dumb and ugly, and because of that, inferior. I was not a competitor and I had no idea what goals were, much less had any.

Toward the end of my formal schooling, I did two semesters of 9B English. I was beginning my third semester of 10B English when the teacher said to me, "Mr. Davis, given that you have been in this class for so long, you do not have to pay the school fee." I saved some money there, and soon after dropped out to join the war effort.

Working for Money

My first paying job was when I was fifteen, working for a horticulturist whom someone told me needed a helper. I walked a mile to where he lived and grew flowers for sale. Given the war and the draft of men eighteen and over, with seventeen-year-olds being able to volunteer, he was happy to find anyone to help him.

The first assignment he gave me was to go down by the creek and hoe the mums. He handed me a hoe and I set off to fulfill the task. About twenty minutes later, he decided to check on my progress. I was doing well with the exception that I took his instruction literally and had by his arrival cut down two-thirds of a row of mums. I think at that time he realized just what he had hired. I have to give him credit: he never said a critical word, just took the hoe and showed me what he had intended me to do. He left me with the rest of the task, which I did well.

The workday was seven to six with a half day on Saturday. I made a dollar a day with full pay for the half day.

I was so proud at the end of the first week when he handed me six one-dollar bills. I walked home feeling very proud and anxious to show those bills to my mother. She was in the kitchen when I got home—I can still recall the event clearly these seventy-some years later—and I rushed in holding the cash and handed it to her to feel. She looked at it for a few minutes and said, "I am so proud of you, Paul, and I think you should keep a dollar of this for yourself." It never occurred to me to argue. We were living in hard times.

Spring Glen Methodist Church

At fourteen, I joined the Boy Scouts at Spring Glen Methodist Church and became a junior assistant Scoutmaster.

At sixteen, I became more involved in the church and was ordained as an exhorter. With all of this, I never got past my low self-esteem and sense of shyness. An interesting memory of my exhorter service began when the pastor asked me to give the sermon at prayer meeting. I agreed and chose the Sermon on the Mount as my topic. Not any one thought or any one theme, but the whole thing.

I learned that it is far easier to start a sermon than it is to stop it. But I finally found an end and I called on an old saint sitting in the first row to close with prayer. He probably would have been happy to end it with a ball bat. But he rose and prayed: "Lord, we thank you for this young man, and we thank you for this discourse on Your Word. A bit long perhaps, but thank you just the same."

I learned that it is easy to start a speech but it is essential that you have a closing statement to use at any point.

Mr. Sikes was the Scoutmaster and was the producer of a weekly newspaper published in South Jacksonville. He urged me to work in his office as a "printer's devil" after school. My main job was to keep the type fonts organized, sweep the floors and do any other task that came to mind. It was a good learning experience for me.

Dr. Pepper Bottling Company

At the end of the summer, already having given up on school, my friend Lee Shows and I found jobs with Dr. Pepper Bottling Company. The pay was $1 per hour, for a forty-hour week. Most of the money went to my family, but I still thought I was rich. After a short period, I became the manager's assistant and was in charge of mixing the materials that were to be bottled.

I still used the bus for transportation and it was going home on the bus one afternoon that I had a life-changing experience. Remember as you read this that I lived and worked in the Deep South where segregation was "wrong but strong."

One afternoon when I got on the bus, it was crowded with only two open seats at the very back of the bus. The area held four seats and was reserved for "colored." There were two whites in the seats and I took the third. A little farther on, a "colored woman" (1939 vernacular) got on the bus, came to the back and asked me if she could take the empty seat.

I was surprised and without thought said no. This left her standing in the aisle with her purse, holding the overhead rail. There I was, sixteen years old, totally unprepared for the event and knowing I was wrong, but still I did not correct the situation.

After several miles, the bus reached her stop and without a word or a look, she got off the bus. I felt a relief at her going, but that in no way helped the embarrassment I had caused for myself. And, truth be known, I still feel embarrassment as I write these words, some seventy-odd years later. I decided at that point never to be guilty again of racist thoughts, words or actions. And this decision worked out for my good when I first went aboard a Liberty ship to take supplies across the Atlantic to England.

Chapter 2

MY WAR EFFORT

Merchant Marines

After Dr. Pepper I worked at Gibbs Shipyard for a while helping to build Liberty ships, the workhorses of the war supply chain. I had no idea at the time that I would very soon be sailing in this kind of ship.

One day my next-door neighbor and close friend Jimmie Rydel came to my house to say that he just learned that sixteen-year-olds could go to maritime school in St. Petersburg, Florida, and then be qualified to work on the oceangoing ships carrying supplies to the war zones.

His dad took us to join the merchant marine, and we were bussed to St. Petersburg. While we learned the most basic facts of what would be expected of us, we seldom saw each other, and when we graduated, Jimmie went somewhere and I was sent to New Orleans, still sixteen, with a very few dollars in my pocket. They did not last long. Getting assigned to a ship was delayed for some reason: I was on my own in an infamous city.

For the first few nights I received food and slept in the Service Men's Center because my uniform looked a lot like the navy uniforms. When they learned that I was merchant marine and not navy, I was asked to leave and found myself on the streets with no place to sleep and practically no money to buy food.

At some point, a total stranger, I guess sensing my confusion, began to talk with me. After some minutes of conversation, he made an offer to let me use his shower, then get some rest and then get some food. Or, that's what I thought.

After a bit, we went to his room, which was nice and clean. He let me have a bath, which felt so good after several days without one. He suggested I lie down while he showered and then we could take a nap, after which we would go down to get dinner. I did so and was half-asleep when he came out of the shower nude. At that same moment, some friends of his knocked on the door, opened it and came in. They recognized what was about to happen and told me to get up and put on some clothes and we would all go to dinner. I have always believed that God delivered me that day from a fate that would have had a very negative effect on my life.

Since I was still waiting for a ship, the Port Office manager advanced me a little money so I could pay for a room and my meals. I met up with one of the guys from training, and we waited for a ship together—there were lots of boats needing crew but they could only put a few recruits on any given boat. My friend suggested we go back to Jacksonville and get assigned to a ship there. I gladly agreed.

We went to the Army Air Forces base and got a ride as far as a base in the western part of Alabama. We then began to walk, hoping for a ride. We walked carrying our sea bags with all of our possessions until well after dark. We got as far as the edge of a small town and, exhausted, with not enough money for a room, we laid down on the sidewalk with our sea bags as pillows. Sometime later a trucker saw us and our uniforms, stopped, woke us up, put our bags in the back and took us to Birmingham, Alabama. From there we took a bus to Jacksonville.

That bus trip ended one of the most trying periods of my life. But at the same time that whole period taught me to grow up and think before acting. I never saw my friend again after that and have no idea as to what his life turned out to be.

When I got off the bus in Jacksonville, I asked a cab driver what it would cost to take me home to Ryar Road. He said $4 and my heart sank. But when I told him I only had $2 left, he said, "Get in, I'll take you home." I was truly glad to be with my family again, even for a short while.

A few weeks later, I went to the local office where merchant seamen were assigned to ships and received my first assignment.

When I was to leave for my first ship, some of my friends decided to have a going-away party for me. At the party Jackie Newton, a neighbor, asked me to go for a walk with her. As shy as I was about girls, I went with her. I am not sure but I believe I held her hand as we walked down a very dark road. I must have said at least a few words but I am not sure.

After walking for a while, we turned back toward the party. About halfway back, she said stop a minute. I did and was surprised when she turned toward me, put her arms around my neck and began to kiss me over and over again. It was as close as I had come to heaven up to that time.

Did I tell you I was shy? That was my first kiss from a girl.

When it was time for me to board the ship, Lee Shows drove me to the pier where it was docked. After some sad good-byes he left me to go aboard and begin a totally different life than I had ever known. I carried my sea bag up the gangplank where I saw a young man sitting on the hold cover. I introduced myself and my job as wiper (also referred to as the lowest thing on a ship that comes from a woman). He told me that he was the other wiper, so we had some common ground. In the course of our conversation he asked me if I knew that the deck engineer was black and that our bunks were in his room. He then asked me what we were to do.

This is where my stupid event with the lady on the bus came rushing back into my mind and the answer I gave him was, "I don't know about you but I am going to sleep in that room and pay him full respect for his position." He said, "Then I guess I will too." It was a wise decision because the deck engineer became a father figure to us, showing absolute patience with two ignorant kids who did not know the bow from the stern.

My first trip was to England with a ship whose holds were filled with cargo and decks filled with tanks and planes to replace those being destroyed in the war. We did have a few submarine scares but overall it was an uneventful journey.

My brother Charles, whom I was closer to than my other siblings, had originally volunteered for the navy, but he had a heart murmur that disqualified him. He joined the merchant marine and had made two trips to England before I was old enough for maritime school. His first ship was torpedoed and sunk on his return trip to the United States. He was rescued by a Canadian Corvette and taken to Canada where they sent him home. His second ship crashed into the rocks off Scotland in a storm. He and the rest of the crew were rescued by Scottish longboat civilians who risked their lives rowing out in the storm time after time to bring all the crew to safety on shore. Charlie returned to the States on the Queen Mary with thousands more in his same position. It was hard for him to get his third assignment because all merchant seamen thought he was jinxed.

Charlie was home when I returned and I suggested that we get our next trip together. Charlie was dead set against the idea. His reasoning was that when we heard the alarm button, he needed to get to his position and if I was there, he would be concerned about me and place his own life at risk.

I finally convinced him, with my mother's help, that we could go together.

Before Charlie and I boarded our ship, some of the girls at Glendale Community Church decided to have a going-away hot dog roast. The night was chosen, the fire built and the hot dogs ready to cook over the open fire. When the party was nearing the end, one of the girls said, "Let's all line up and kiss Charlie good-bye." They did and Charlie enjoyed every minute of it.

I was sitting off to the side and not one girl even came to say good-bye, much less kiss me good-bye.

Talk about confirmation of dumb and ugly.

I told that story for years after the war and laughed with the listeners. But one day I was visiting with my psychologist and told him the story. To my surprise, I found myself crying. He waited until I dried my eyes and said, "You have been carrying that hurt around for a lot of years." True, but the cry helped to overcome the hurt.

Back to the story: Charlie and I boarded our ship in Jacksonville. Given our common positions as wipers, we both slept in the room with the deck engineer. Charlie got the top bunk and I had the bottom. (This is jumping way ahead but one night in the Pacific, the alarm sounded. I sat up and as I did I felt Charlie brush against my head and go through the door at a dead run. When I got to the stern, where we served as loaders for the 20 mm cannons manned by navy personnel, I stopped just long enough to tell Charlie how much I appreciated his concern for me. He just laughed as did all others nearby.)

We left Jacksonville for New Orleans to load cargo. We left New Orleans to sail through the gulf and down to Panama where we went through the Panama Canal to the Pacific and then after several stops in the war zone, we traveled to the Philippines; first at the Invasion of Lingayen Gulf and shortly thereafter to Manila for that invasion.

After unloading our cargo in Manila, we left shortly for our journey back to California and then up to Seattle to disembark. Charlie and I joined two crewmembers for a car trip across the country to Birmingham, Alabama, where Charlie and I caught a bus for the rest of our journey.

One of the things I learned on this trip was the "ready, fire, aim" approach to reaching a target. This was years before Tom Peters came on the scene.

My task was to place a round canister of cannon shells in the opening made for it on the cannon. The navy gunner strapped himself into the harness, pulled back the handgrip to load the first shell and all of the others followed from the recoil until the last shell was fired. At that point, I removed the empty canister and replaced it with a full canister as quickly as possible.

The gunner aimed by pointing the gun as near as possible to the enemy plane and pulled the trigger. Every third round in the canister was a phosphorescent cartridge that left a trail of smoke behind the round. The gunner then moved the smoke trail to a point in front of the speeding plane. Hence the expression "ready, fire, aim."

When I began to build Paul W. Davis Systems, Inc., I soon found that you first need to have a target and that the best way to get there was to start doing as much as you knew and keep making small adjustments as you moved toward your goal. Thus, before it became big news in the business world, the ready-fire-aim strategy certainly paid big dividends for me.

A word of caution: You can't get to where you want to go if you aren't sure *where* you want to go.

When Charlie and I returned, I fully expected to sail again. I knew the risk but I loved being a part of the ships delivering much-needed materials to our frontline fighters. They were the greatest risk takers.

It was a second blessing that we were paid by the day but had no place to spend the money.

Army

But my best friend, Lee Shows, was now eighteen, and had been called up for the draft into the army.

I had the bright idea that I would volunteer and go with him. I was accepted and we were put on a train and taken to Camp Blanding, Florida, for indoctrination. We both passed and were put on a train to go to Atlanta, Georgia. We were taken off the train, and Lee went to one barracks and I went to another.

It was the last time I saw Lee until we were discharged at the end of the war. (Did I mention dumb?)

The one good thing that came of the Camp Blanding experience was that we were required to take an IQ test. We were told the average grade was 110 and my score was 121. Hearing that score gave me my first taste of self-esteem and it felt *so good*. It did not guarantee that I would not do dumb stuff, but it did help me to understand that I was not stupid.

From Atlanta, I was sent to North Carolina for Basic Training. I found that I enjoyed the army although I was confused by some of their regulations.

At one point I was assigned to guard duty for a night. It was snowing and bitter cold, especially for a Florida boy. But I made my hours, was brought back to the barracks, told where to place my rifle and given a cot to sleep on.

When I woke up, I looked for my rifle and couldn't find it. Someone else had taken it instead of their own. The sergeant sent me back to my unit where I was asked where my rifle was. I explained the problem and was told, "Your rifle is your responsibility and there is no acceptable excuse for your losing it." My punishment was to serve KP (kitchen police) from eight to midnight for two weeks. I did so without complaint.

At some point, a notice was posted that anyone who wished to apply for Officer Training was to notify the company clerk, who would help with the paperwork. I did and his response was, "Paul you can't qualify for Officer Training. You have to have a minimum IQ of 110 and yours is only 95."

I replied that my IQ was 121, but he said, "Don't argue with me, I have the records."

Two weeks later, when it was too late to apply, that clerk stopped me near his office and said, "Paul you were right, I looked at the IQ of the Paul Davies file."

Not even an apology for looking up the wrong name and by that, denying me the chance to go through Officer Training. But in retrospect I can see God's hand in that screw-up because He had other, far better plans for my life.

When Basic Training was over, I was assigned to a bakery unit to wait for transfer. I was put in charge of a unit of four men whose task was to keep the bakery equipment working. Having no skill for my assigned task, I was moved about and finally was placed in charge of a warehouse where excess furniture was stored.

That led to an interesting event.

My mother wrote me and in the letter asked, "Paul, what do you do in the army?"

If you have tried to read my handwriting, you know it is not good. But back then it was almost unreadable. Nevertheless, I wrote back with my poor spelling and said, "I manage a warehouse, Momma."

A few months later I went home on furlough. When Momma had a chance to get me alone she said, "Paul, tell me exactly what it is you do in the army." I said, "I manage a warehouse Momma." Her sigh of relief could probably have been heard even next door.

On my return to service, I was working at something in front of our barracks when an officer walked by. He looked at me and asked, "Where are your PFC stripes, Davis?" I answered, "Sir, I am still a private." He shook his head and said, "Did we promote that damned Davies?" I said, "Yes sir, you did." I got my PFC stripe the next day.

The war ended shortly thereafter and the process of reducing the size of the military began. The real heroes, those who fought the battles, were the most important. Soldiers like me, who never finished training, were targeted for discharge as well.

Chapter 3
MY WORKING
LIFE BEGINS

Loyce Watkins Changes My Direction

And so I came home from my army service and a short time later I was introduced to Loyce Watkins. Three months later we were married. I honestly can't remember ever having an actual date until I was introduced to Loyce by one of my cousins. We were married by the Methodist pastor who had been such a powerful influence for good to me. And Lee Shows and his soon-to-be wife stood up for us. Lee had a car, so after the ceremony he dropped us off at our garage apartment in an alley between Second and Third streets in downtown Jacksonville. And it was home for us for our first few years. Loyce worked for Bell South and I worked for a printing company specializing in business cards.

My job was to place a blank business card in the press, wait for the press to close and make the imprint, remove the printed card and replace it with another blank card. The total process took a lot less time than it has taken you to read this description. And it was utter boredom hour after hour, day after day.

I really did not like the work or the hours so I took time to go to the Veterans Administration to see if they could help me to understand what sort of work I should be looking for. They gave me a series of tests and said that I should be looking for work as a salesman.

Mason Lumber Company

It just so happened that one of my childhood idols was Mr. Braxton (Brack) Newton, who was vice-president of sales at Mason Lumber Company. I called Mr. Newton and asked him if they needed a salesman. He said yes we do and we need some trainees also. I got his message, recognized that there had to be a starting point for me, and told him I would like to apply for a training position. He suggested I come for an interview for a job in the lumber and building supplies department, as it offered more opportunities than did the millwork division that he directed. So I took the bus to the office, which was on Edison Avenue on the opposite side of town from where Loyce and I lived.

I met with the desk manager and was then taken to Mr. Mason's office. After a few minutes of conversation, he stood up and started out of his office. Not knowing what to do, I followed him down the hall and through a self-closing door. I then knew why he left the office: I stood there red-faced as he urinated.

Not the best introduction, but when we came out he said, "Come in Monday and see Mr. Alexander. He'll tell you what to do."

I did so and was introduced to Mr. Torbert to learn about materials and pricing. That turned out to be one of the most important watershed events of my life. He gave me the foundation on which all of my accomplishments were built.

His job was to check every invoice for accuracy. He used an electric comptometer (amazing for its day). I used a hand-operated calculator and worked on the smaller invoices.

I spent my lunch hour walking through the entire operation, one complete city block, from sawmill to concrete block to sales departments. I worked hard to learn as much as I could on my own and take full advantage of any help I could get from those who had been there for years.

The purpose in assigning me to Mr. Torbert was to teach me while taking some of the workload off him and giving it to me.

Working with him accomplished two things: it prepared me to work with customers if and when the opportunity arose, and it showed Mr. Alexander, the vice-president of sales, that I could be taught to work as an inside sales person.

One Monday morning, a desk salesman failed to show up for work because he had spent the weekend on a drunken binge. Mr. Alexander called and told him he was fired and was not to come back into the building. He had a couple of prospects, but when Mr. Torbert heard the news, he went to the desk and convinced Mr. Alexander to give me the position.

Then came the hard part: convincing *me* that I could do the job. I was scared to death, but finally agreed to try. Mr. Alexander and the other salesman were very patient and helpful. But, as time passed, they pushed me more and more to be on my own. I worked hard, continued to study every item we offered for sale and developed several customers who only wanted me to serve them. I was very pleased to have the position and be paid $75 per week instead of the $55 per week I was making.

Sometime later, Mr. Mason heard about a six-week training course in Atlanta. It was sponsored by a group of wholesale companies, many of whom supplied Mason Lumber Company. He talked with my boss, Mr. Alexander, and they agreed that I should go. My brother Bob and his wife Sally lived in Atlanta and they suggested I stay with them rather than the hotels chosen by the sponsors. It required a long bus trip each day but I enjoyed being with them and probably evaded some pretty rough partying evenings.

It was an amazing six weeks, and I learned a great deal about a range of materials that stood me in good stead as new opportunities arose. I had no idea at the time, but that six weeks prepared me for some important promotions as time passed.

Working for Mason Lumber Company was a nine-hour-a-day, five-days-plus-five-hours-on-Saturday job. Add to that the fact I worked through lunches and spent a minimum of thirty minutes on a bus morning and night all six days, and I felt I was working flat-out.

At some point during all of this, I decided that I needed to at least get my high school diploma. Remember I had failed ninth grade and then dropped out of school to get involved in the war. To cover my reluctance to admit that I was a school dropout, I learned to say, when the question was raised, that I had skipped two grades in high school. I never bothered to say that those grades were eleven and twelve.

I went to night school for three weeks and my teacher, knowing about my various wartime experiences and that I had an IQ of 121, decided that given all of that I had earned at least a high school diploma. She came to me and said, "You have earned this." I knew she was referring to my wartime service and I accepted the diploma with much appreciation.

My work continued and I learned more about the total operation as time passed. But I felt stuck at Mason Lumber Company, because of the pay and the fact I didn't have a company car, and began to look for a different job. My brother Bob, who was a very successful specialist for Nabisco, was visiting the local office and in a conversation with the manager there discovered that he was looking to hire a new salesman.

Bob told him about me and the manager asked him to have me come for an interview. Bob talked with me; I called and made an appointment that led to a very good interview. At the close of the meeting, the manager said, "You are what we need. I will call you as soon as the position is open." I truly believe that I walked on air in my excitement and anticipation.

The position was a dream job to me:

- the pay was $450 per month. I was making $325 per month at Mason Lumber Company
- a car and gas was furnished and could be driven for personal as well as business use
- the job was five days per week rather than five-and-a-half days

- Nabisco provided health insurance. I had none.

To me, at age twenty-two, this was the equivalent of dying a painless death and going directly to heaven. Soon after that meeting, Loyce and I went on a one-week vacation. While we were away the Nabisco manager called Mason Lumber Company and asked to speak with me.

When told that I was on vacation, he asked to speak to Mr. Newton, who was a personal friend of his. In the conversation, Mr. Newton ask why he had called. The Nabisco manager told him that he had called to tell me he was ready for me to start work. Mr. Newton responded that I wasn't there, but my brother Charlie was and he would make a great salesman for Nabisco. The manager said to send him over.

When Loyce and I returned, Charlie was a Nabisco salesman and I was still at Mason Lumber Company. I felt no anger toward Charlie, since he had no idea I had interviewed for the job.

Was I disappointed? Absolutely! But I continued at Mason Lumber Company and in retrospect learned more of the Bible truth, "And we know that all things work together for good to them that love God, to them who are the called according to His purpose" (Romans 8:28, KJV).

Had I gone to Nabisco, I would probably have spent the balance of my life there. They are a great company to work for.

Green Cove Springs Company

One day Mr. Mason came to the sales desk to announce that he had just bought a small lumber and supply company in Green Cove Springs, Florida, about thirty miles south of Jacksonville. Much to my surprise, he said he wanted me to manage the Green Cove Springs company.

I was both shocked and elated at the offer of a promotion to branch manager at the age of twenty-five, and after some assurance of help from Mr. Alexander I agreed.

Mr. Mason said, "Paul you will be highly respected by the businesspeople in Green Cove Springs. They will want you to become a member of Rotary, and be seen as a leader in the community. We will furnish you with a car, your gas and still pay you what you make now plus ten percent of each year's profit."

I was so excited about my first promotion that I never thought to question the offer.

At the appointed time, I went to Green Cove Springs and met the two employees who were responsible for receiving and storing materials, helping customers to find what they wanted and seeing that it got delivered. The office, the salesroom and all in-house stored materials were my responsibility as well as creating the invoices, collecting the money and banking.

For the first six months, I drove the thirty miles morning and night (in the furnished car, an old 1939 Model A Ford). During that time, we bought a lot and built an 880-square-foot home that cost us $8,800 for the house and lot. Once the house was finished we moved and Loyce continued her work in Jacksonville, sharing a ride with a gentleman we met in Green Cove Springs, who also worked in Jacksonville. It was a different world back then and trusting people was the norm and seldom a risk.

I was invited to and accepted by Rotary, became a director and eventually president. I was also elected chair of the local American Red Cross chapter, and held positions in other service clubs.

The business continued to grow and I saw less and less of Mr. Mason. He did come at the end of each year to review our progress and the profits.

I remember well one of these yearly visits. I was proud of the good year we had and was happy to see him when he came for his review. We'd made a good profit of which I would receive ten percent. I thought our collections were good: we had to write off less than one percent of sales to bad collection. When we came to the point of the meeting where I could enjoy feeling proud of the low number, Mr. Mason said, "Well OK Paul, but let's try to do better next year."

Mr. Mason was old school but he was one of the finest men I have ever known. I made no effort to emulate him because it would not have worked for me. I still look back on our relationship with appreciation for his trust and the positive impact he had on my young life.

Brackridge Paint and Hardware in Tiger Hole

A few years later, my brother Bob called to tell me that Mr. Newton, my mentor, idol and my brother Bob's father-in-law, had left Mason Lumber Company and was building a housing development on his property. He had named the development Tiger Hole.

Bob said that Mr. Newton wanted me to come and manage a paint, hardware and appliance store, from which he would purchase all of these materials. That would guarantee me sales, and I would get $75 per week, plus one third of the profit. I gave up my current job—$100 per week, plus car and gas, plus ten percent of the profits—and said yes, believing we could not fail.

Unknown to me there was one issue that concerned Mr. Newton, and that was the fact that I smoked. I had no idea that this was an issue until later.

My mother and father came to spend a weekend with Loyce and me. My father wanted to go to church on Sunday. I seldom went, but agreed to take him because it was such an important part of his life. We woke late and left as soon as possible so as not to be late.

I don't remember the sermon subject but when it was over, we got up and followed the crowd out the front door. The norm for me was to light a smoke as I went down the steps. But for some reason, out of the blue, the thought came to me, "I have not had a smoke this far today, why not wait until after lunch?" After lunch, I again reached for a smoke and the weird thought came again, "Why not wait until after dinner?" After dinner, the same thought and the same reaction,

"Well, why not make it a day?" So I did, and I didn't smoke again for many years.

It was later when Bob heard that I had given up smoking that he called me and told me that Mr. Newton was bothered by my smoking and hoped that I would give it up. The Newton family had a custom that the entire family met every Saturday night at the Newton home for a prayer meeting. Bob said the night before I gave up smoking, the entire prayer time was dedicated to asking God to take away my desire to smoke. They asked, God answered and I, not having the slightest idea about what was going on, gave up smoking. I still have, almost sixty years later, the absolute belief that my giving up smoking truly was a result of that prayer meeting.

I resigned from my job at Mason Lumber Company. Loyce and I sold our home and moved back to Jacksonville to live in Tiger Hole, in a Brackridge two-bedroom house across the street from my brother Bob and his wife Sally. Mr. Newton opened Brackridge Paint and Hardware on Hogan Road (now Beach Boulevard) and I took responsibility for operations.

At Mason Lumber Company, I was furnished a car and was paid $100 per week, plus a percentage of the profit. At Brackridge Paint and Hardware, I was paid $75 per week, supplied my own car and paid for my own gas.

But that was OK, because I had a guaranteed customer who would make the business profitable. Or so I thought.

A short time after I moved, Duval County passed a law that all multi-home developments would require a very expensive system for water and sewage disposal—no more single wells and septic tanks. Mr. Newton had no funding to meet the new standards and therefore had to give the property to Mason Lumber Company to pay his bills. And he immediately closed Brackridge Paint and Hardware. I was out of a job.

Florida Lumber and Supply

After one of the shortest employment periods of my life—six weeks—
my mentor Mr. Newton pulled a rabbit out of his hat for both of us.
He called Ted Floyd, a friend at Florida Lumber and Supply, who also
happened to be the owner. Mr. Newton explained our situation and
his friend agreed to hire both of us.

My salary was $75 per week, for five-and-a-half days. I furnished
my own car and gas for the roughly fifteen miles there and back per
day. Looking at the previous three months, the best label I could put
on it was that I was "failing my way up the ladder of success."

I was the leader of the young people from the junior and senior
high schools at our church. Each year, Columbia Bible College held a
weekend retreat for prospective students and any others who wished
to attend. As the youth leader, I was expected to drive and take as
many kids as possible. Many of our young people chose Columbia
Bible College as a result of these trips. Given that the conference
began Friday evening, I needed that Friday off. I finally got up enough
courage to ask the owner to allow me that day off.

His response was, "Come out to the warehouse with me." I did
and he turned to face me, looked me in the eye and said, curse words
omitted, "Paul, you know this business and you could be a great help
to me, but you are making me and everyone else around you misera-
ble. You are acting like a real jack*** moping around feeling sorry for
yourself. I am not responsible for your misfortune of giving up a good
job that paid more money than I can pay you.

"You came to me and asked for a job and I gave you one. I hired
you because Mr. Newton recommended you. I admit you do what has
to be done, but you don't do one bit more. And because of the way
you act, I hate to come into my own business. All you do is sulk over
your problems, treat my customers with disrespect and let my office
get cluttered and dirty. So you can go, but don't come back unless you
can change your 'poor me' outlook."

Was this a tough message? Yes! How did I feel? Humiliated, shocked, embarrassed and ashamed. Was it true? Absolutely. I felt about two inches high. My ego was bruised and my pride hurt, but he brought me face to face with the reality that I was not a victim, that I had made good choices that did not work out well, and that I was literally punishing everyone around me as a result.

My response was, "I will come back. I don't know how long I will stay, but I promise you that when I go, you will wish I could stay."

I made the trip and returned to work determined to change my attitude:

- treat every person who walked through the doors with utmost respect
- clean and organize the sales office
- clean and organize the entire warehouse.

After I got all of that done, I thanked him for all he had done for me. And told him I had to find a place to make more money to support my family.

He said, "Paul, you were right. I really do wish you could stay, but I can't afford to pay you more."

I still recognize that episode as being a down and dirty, quick and powerful watershed event in my young life. I learned in the course of a five-minute conversation that allowing myself to accept the role of victim would lead only to total self-destruction. I learned that I have the sole right to determine my attitude. I learned that my future depended to a large degree on how I reacted to my past. I will always appreciate what Ted Floyd did for me on that day. He gave a jackass the key that would allow it to become a thoroughbred if it so desired.

The whole experience taught me that my productivity should never be based on my income. But I also learned to find work where, as much as practical, my income was based on my productivity. Whatever compensation you have agreed to calls for 100 percent of your ability and effort to reach your employer's goals.

From that day, my actions changed and my hope was restored. I began to see the future in an entirely different light. I felt a measure of control over my destiny that I had never felt before. I recognized that while I could not control the people around me or the circumstances of my life, I was the only one who could control my mindset, and that this was the absolute key to my destiny.

And so I swallowed my pride and went back to Mason Lumber Company to find a job.

Mason Lumber Company, Part Two

Mr. Mason had died and his oldest son, Bill, had taken his position as president.

Bill greeted me warmly and when I explained my experience after leaving Green Cove Springs, he agreed to hire me as an outside salesman at $75 per week, plus gas and upkeep for my car for a five-and-a-half-day week.

I spent most of my time working in the office, helping contractors and wannabe contractors to understand the materials they would need for specific jobs and what they would cost. I could do that because several years back, when I was first working at the sales desk, I went to see Mr. Newton and asked him if he would teach me how to read blueprints and estimate the materials needed for each job.

He agreed, and turned to a stack of blueprints and handed one set to me. He then said, "Take these home and do the best job you can. I will review what you have done and help you with the errors." I did as he instructed me to do and was amazed at how much I could calculate based on the knowledge I had acquired working at the sales desk.

He helped me with several issues, the most important one of which was that I was never to estimate electrical, plumbing or heating and air-conditioning, which were specialties that required licensed individuals.

One of the personal benefits I received from that knowledge was totally unexpected.

Earl Huffingham, a member of the Sunday school class I taught, was a Gideon and he wanted me to become a Gideon also. The catch was that there was a $15 fee to join. Given that I was the sole support for my wife Loyce and our two children, Debra and Mary Susan, there were no extra funds available.

One Saturday morning, a stranger knocked on my door and said he needed someone to estimate how much and what kinds of material he would need to do a job he had undertaken. I asked him to come in and took his blueprints and wrote out the material needs. It did not take long and he asked what he owed me. The thought that came to mind was the Gideon membership and I said $15. He asked was I sure that was enough and I said yes. That was not fair to my wife and children, but it did allow me to serve God through the Gideons for some time.

Now back to my return to Mason Lumber Company. At that time, Prudential Insurance Company had opened a regional office in South Jacksonville and moved hundreds of workers to Jacksonville.

One day, one of the Prudential Insurance Company executives came into Mason Lumber Company wanting prices on materials he would need to have a home built. He was referred to me and after some discussion, he left his house plans with me and we set a date for him to return for my quote. He told me the names of two other companies that were doing the same thing for him. Knowing this I also knew that we would be outbid because Mason Lumber Company had a fixed rule that there would be no discounts. Nevertheless, I made an accurate list of materials, priced it out and came to a figure of six thousand dollars plus. That doesn't sound like much in today's market, but it was huge for the home market in that time.

He returned at the agreed time and we went over my list and I gave him the total. He said, "This is the most accurate and understandable list I have received. But both of the other companies are ten percent or more under your price."

At that point a thought came to me, and it made for another of my life's watershed events. I considered it then and I still do now as a thought that came directly through the Holy Spirit of God.

Without further consideration of the consequences of what I was about to say on behalf of Mason Lumber Company, I said, "What if you agree to buy all your materials from us and I will furnish the workers and oversee their work rather than you having to pay a contractor to do that task?"

He did some quick mental calculations and said, "Let's do it."

Over a short period of time, he introduced me and my offer to several other people; I think the total houses built, using this same agreement, was close to ten, which was a lot in that day. Bill Mason did not say a lot, but he knew that this was an "outside of the box" approach and gave his full approval. I would have appreciated a raise more.

Not too long thereafter, I was appointed manager of the South Jacksonville Operations of Mason Lumber Company. Finally, this included a raise that brought me back to the salary I had in Green Cove Springs five years earlier.

Sometime later one of my desk clerks came to me and asked, "Did you know that the company is building houses in South Jacksonville [which was our territory] and all the materials are furnished by the main office with us cut off completely?" I admitted that I did not.

I called Bill Mason and told him that this was totally unfair as it reduced our sales and even more, it reduced my year-end bonus. He responded, in effect, that it was a company decision and would not be changed.

As I look back, I see it as another "God thing" that moved me a step closer toward God's ultimate plan for my life.

Life Insurance Sales

Somewhere I saw an advertisement for prospective life insurance agents for Sun Life Insurance Company of Canada. I decided to apply, did so, and was accepted as a prime prospect—another proof of how far wrong management can be in selecting prospects. I submitted my letter of resignation to Bill Mason and began the two-year training process during which I had a guaranteed income equal to my gross income at Mason Lumber Company.

I sold very little insurance, but that was not my fault. The fault lay with those people who knew they needed life insurance but would not take the time to find out who I was, where I was and that I really wanted to help them, if they would just call me.

A friend of mine worked as an agent for a general agent who represented a company located in North Carolina. He suggested that I come by his office and meet his general agent. I did so and his general agent hired me to supervise his agents.

Naturally, I did not do any better job as a supervisor than I had as an agent. But a vice president of an insurance company in Birmingham, Alabama, somehow got my name, called me and came out to see me. After some discussion, he offered me a position as manager of an agency I was to build. He guaranteed me $400 per month for up to two years. I signed the contract.

Obviously, I was no better a general manager than I was an agent or a supervisor. But I was, it seemed at the time, repeatedly failing my way up the ladder of success.

Chapter 4

THE MOVE TO INSURANCE RESTORATION CONTRACTING

My First Taste

I had a very good friend, Bob Schroeder, who was a general contractor building new homes. I rode with him often as he made his rounds, which provided me an escape from my office, a continual reminder of my ongoing failure as an insurance salesman. Visiting job sites with Bob was also the platform on which God began the process of moving me out of life insurance into what ultimately became Paul W. Davis Contracting.

One day as we were riding to one of his projects, I suggested that we put an advertisement in the Yellow Pages and when we got responses, I would go out to see the owners, list the work to be done, price it out and get a contract signed. At that point, Bob would take over and get the work done. We would then split the profit. Bob thought it was a good idea that would help each of us in a low business period of our lives. He agreed to contact Yellow Pages and get our advertisement in.

About a week later we were again in his truck and he said we have a problem. The new Yellow Pages have just been sent and will not be revised for at least six months.

I guess I had hoped they'd take our name and go from door to door inserting it in each book.

It was a hard blow to what I had thought would be a perfect solution for both of us. But the saying is true for believers, "When God closes one door, He almost without exception opens another one," as you will see in the following.

Bob said, "I just finished repairing my dentist's office after a fire. The adjuster who handled it for the insurance company was a man named Earl Linder. He said he was very pleased with the way I handled the repairs. And, he said that if I would like to do some of this kind of work, to call him." Bob asked, "Would you be interested in us talking with Earl?" And not having any idea of what insurance restoration was or how it was conducted, I said yes, and Bob agreed to call him.

The next day we went to the office of Linder & Company, Inc. Insurance Adjusters to meet with Earl Linder, find out what his company did and how we could fit into it. Earl talked with us for about thirty minutes to explain his property damage adjusting service for insurers and their policyholders. He asked if we would like to become one of the contractors he recommended to policy-holders who had incurred property damage. Bob, who understood this far better than I did, said yes.

Earl then called for Tom Kline to come in and meet us. And after a few minutes, Earl said to Tom, "When you have a loss, give Bob and Paul a chance to make the repairs, if the property owner agrees." Tom went back to his desk; we shook hands with Earl, thanked him and left.

Neither of us had the slightest idea that a total transformation of our business lives had just taken place. As time went on and we learned the ropes from Tom Kline, I realized that meeting was another one of the major watershed events of my life. And I believed then and I still believe today that it was the work of the Holy Spirit in His direction of my life.

SYFTKOG (Seek ye first the Kingdom of God)

In retrospect, I realize that what transpired that day began in Glendale Community Church some two months prior.

I was sitting with Loyce in Glendale Community Church one evening listening to a professor from Columbia Bible College preach on "Seek ye first the Kingdom of God, and His righteousness; and all these things shall be added unto you." At the close of his sermon, I did not go forward, I did not make a statement, I did not make any outward move. But I committed then to change my approach to life. I would quit trying to succeed and instead begin to seek God's will for my life, and trust Him to give to me all those things that were a part of His will for my life.

I walked out of that church that night with a peace far beyond any I had experienced before and with a determination to place my life in God's hands—to seek His will, not mine.

The morning after our visit with Earl and Tom, Bob had gone to check in with the subcontractors working on the house he was building.

I was in my insurance office. I almost wrote sales office, but I want to keep this factual, so I left out the word sales.

Little Things Mean a Lot

The phone rang and it was Tom Kline. He said he had just been assigned a property loss and would I like to go with him to look at the damages?

I said yes and he said, "Pick me up out front in thirty minutes, and we'll go." I had absolutely no idea of what was about to happen. Nor the fact that God was in the process of turning my entire work life around and placing me in a business that I very quickly learned to love and enjoy.

And so, I picked up Tom and went to the house where the owner had experienced a grease fire. Tom talked with the owner, took some measurements and said to the owner, "You can repair this yourself, have someone else do it or let Mr. Davis repair it for you."

She said the magic words, "Let Mr. Davis do it." Little did she know just how little Mr. Davis knew about the task, but Mr. Kline was the person recommended by her insurer and that was enough for her.

When we got back in the car, Tom gave me his notes. The total amount of the job was $165, and it turned out to be the smallest job I did in all my years in the insurance restoration contracting business. But, it was the life-changing event that was the beginning of a company that is approaching $1B of sales as I write this in December of 2015.

One recent day I heard the very old song, "Little Things Mean a Lot." It made me think of that first $165 sale and the tremendous impact it had on my life, when I had just committed to "Seek ye first the Kingdom of God, and His Righteousness; and all these things shall be added unto you."

God does not lay out our future for us to see and consider. He reveals it moment by moment, the good, the bad and the indifferent. And it is generally in retrospect that we see how the Holy Spirit has brought us to where we are now, for me as I write this and for you as you read it.

Golden Crown Builders, Inc.
Startup Success

The year was 1961; I was 33. Bob and I began to get more and more calls from Tom and from others he recommended us to. We formed a company, Golden Crown Builders, under which we worked together for the next five years. Over time, I did most of the measuring, estimating and sales and Bob, who was an expert general contractor, focused on getting the work done. Each of us did some work in both positions, but our real focus was on the one for which we were best suited.

Our gross sales increased each year, but we never made even a moderate profit. We did not give it a lot of thought because after the business and family bills were paid, we spent most of the money fishing, dining, attending ball games, etc. Was that smart? No! Was it enjoyable? Yes. Our sales increased each year, but we seldom showed a profit at year's end. We were young, we were having fun and the future did not cause us much concern. Aside from enjoying ourselves, during those years Bob taught me much that enabled me to lay the foundation for what is now Paul Davis Restoration, Inc.

A member of the Sunday school class I taught worked as the assistant general manager of the regional federal General Services Administration (GSA), which was responsible for the upkeep and improvement of federally owned or leased buildings and their furnishings. He asked Bob if we would be interested in doing some work for the property his office was responsible for. Bob discussed it with me and it sounded like he had found a great source of business for our company.

We went to meet with our friend and his boss. We quickly caught onto what their needs were. As usual, Bob caught on faster than I did. But when he explained it to me, I knew it was a perfect fit for the estimating program I was developing. What I did was apply the insurance restoration contracting system to this new market. The GSA work quickly turned into a new profit center for Golden Crown Builders, Inc.

The Crown Begins to Tarnish

At some point in our fifth year, Bob's outlook began to change. He had taught me the two markets we served—insurance restoration contracting and the General Services Administration—which he had learned much quicker than I had. I developed the systems but without his knowledge of general contracting, my systems would have had no value.

Over time, the estimating systems were recognized as major improvements in the insurance restoration field and in services contracting in general. I had more than 75 procedures and practices outlined for controlling costs and ensuring profits in all areas of our business, from preparing a scope of loss to contracting tradespeople, to billing accounts receivable.

Bob began to feel left out. My systems were getting attention in the company, and people started to come to me, not Bob. In retrospect, I can see that much of the blame was mine for not making sure that he received the recognition he deserved. Even as I write this, I feel a sense of sadness at the loss of his friendship.

But for the first time in my working life I was getting the recognition and affirmation I had wanted and needed for years. I don't say this as an excuse—there is none—but to help you to understand why I failed Bob when he needed me most.

The Beginning of the End

As things went from bad to worse, I said to Bob one afternoon, "I think it is time for us to split up. My suggestion is for one of us to make an offer to sell and for the other to have the right to sell or buy."

Bob said, "I agree. You make the offer and I will decide to stay or sell." I worked very hard at coming up with a fair agreement, believing that he would choose to sell and then start over. The offer did not call for the seller or the buyer to leave the insurance restoration contracting business. The terms were:

- we would each keep our company car and pay the outstanding auto-loan balance
- whoever sells would get to keep their office desk, chair and calculator
- there would be no restriction on continuing in the insurance restoration contracting business
- the buyer would pay the seller $1,000 in cash and $100 per week for one year.

The Shock of His Choice

The next morning, I gave my proposal to Bob, believing he would sell. He studied the proposal for about fifteen minutes, looked at me and said, "I will buy."

With no signed agreement, I took my personal belongings, my office furniture, my car with its monthly payments and myself out of the office. I was shell-shocked by the fact that I was out of a job.

I did not get the $1,000 cash payment or any of the $100 per week payments. More on that later.

I was not only out of a job; I had no cash reserve. And I had a wife and two daughters to support. I also had a mortgage as well as the car payments.

I knew that I wanted to stay in the insurance restoration contracting business, but was not sure just how to do that.

Chapter 5
PAUL W. DAVIS
CONTRACTING

My Wake-Up Message

It was three days after Bob and I parted ways that I awoke in the morning and, still lying in bed for a few minutes, had the thought that I believe was a message direct from the Holy Spirit.

The thought was, What if I sold a job for $1,000 and I could get the work done (labor and material) for $650. I would have $350 net per week for business expenses, and a fair amount to live on.

After breakfast, I went to the South Jacksonville Mason Lumber Company office, which was managed by my mentor, Mr. Newton.

I also saw a painter who had worked with us at Golden Crown Builders, Inc. I spoke to him and asked, "John, if I were to sell a painting job for $1,000, would you furnish the materials and labor and do the job for $650?" He thought a minute and said yes.

Later I saw a carpenter whom I had worked with. I asked the same question using the same figures and he said yes. My early morning thought had proven to be practical.

A little later, I asked Mr. Newton, "If I buy my materials from you, will you let me build an office in your warehouse and operate from there?" He said yes.

The foundation for the Paul Davis Restoration, Inc. of today came into being first as God planted it in my mind, and then through the acceptance of the operational plan by the core tradesmen who would put it into action.

Starting Over: Paul W. Davis Contracting

The basic plan of operation was finished and the groundwork laid. My hope was to meet that projected $1,000 per week, but God had other plans. It was 1966. Knowing unit pricing and insurance restoration estimating from my five years with Golden Crown Builders, Inc. gave me a reference point from which to sell jobs at a very fair price. My definition of a fair price then and still today is, "The lowest equitable price which will provide quality workmanship to the property owner, fair compensation to the tradesman, fair profit to the corporation, and low cost to the insurer."

The next day, I got a call from one of my former adjuster clients. He told me about a fire that happened just five blocks from my home. He asked me to meet the owner, make an estimate and do whatever needed to be done. I met with the owner who authorized me to make the repairs, made a scope of the loss and made arrangements for the restoration to begin the next day. The total job came to more than $12,000—twelve times what I had hoped to bill each week, and twelve times the $350 I needed to operate the business and pay myself. I exceeded my target. The next week a tornado passed through Orange Park and Tom Kline asked me to go with him to survey the damages to three houses assigned to him. We went; we made the estimates, and Tom urged me to take only one job, because otherwise I could get behind and lose my business. I agreed; again the job was a little over $12,000. The last eight months of the year when I started Paul W. Davis Contracting, I did $194,000 of business and that was just the starting point. It was 1966; I was thirty-eight years old and I renamed the business Paul W. Davis Contracting, Inc.

The plan of operation God placed in my mind worked perfectly, and I knew as soon as a job was sold, how much profit it would produce.

Some Basic Lessons Learned Early

One of the things I learned very quickly in the insurance restoration contracting business was that in that era, the 1960s, contractors in general were not held in high esteem. This was long before contractors were required to pass an exam, obtain a license and provide proof of insurance. And of course the honest, hard-working dependable contractors paid the price of being distrusted as a result.

It was this reputation that caused me to endeavor to present myself in a different light. I always wore a dress shirt and a tie with properly pressed trousers, and in winter I wore a suit with a coat and tie. Was I out of place in a coat and tie? Was I out of place in the mud, muck and mire, as a part of insurance restoration work? Yes! But that was one of my strengths in differentiating Paul W. Davis Contracting, Inc. from the norm.

I refused to drive pickup trucks because they were a part of the contractor image I was trying to avoid.

All of this was a part of what became a Paul Davis Systems mantra: "Paul Davis Systems is not about doing things better, Paul Davis Systems is about doing things differently to achieve a better result."

I remember one incident, where having been assigned a loss to estimate, I went to the badly burned and heavily smoked house to perform the task. The owner was there, trying to salvage what could be salvaged. She answered my knock on the door and after I introduced myself and my mission, she invited me in.

As I was performing my walk-through and recording the work required, she stopped what she was doing, looked at how I was dressed and said, "You sure don't look like a contractor." My reply was to smile and say thank you. I did not get a work authorization signed for that job, but it was not because of how I was dressed, it was because the owner had a family friend who was in the same business as I was.

When I began to add estimators and salespeople to Paul Davis Contracting and later as I taught new franchisees, I always stressed my willingness to be different by saying to them, "I don't want you to look like, act like or smell like a contractor." I urged them to think of themselves as a businessman or businesswoman selling a contracting service. I also urged them not to drive pickup trucks, because at that time they were a part of the image I sought to avoid.

Of course, as I am writing this almost fifty years later, the pickup truck issue is no longer valid, but appearance is still a major factor concerning your drive for success. Your prospect knows nothing about you except to some degree the purpose of your visit. In today's insurance restoration contracting business environment, informal dress is acceptable even at home office levels. But even today, your overall appearance is a factor in how much credibility your message carries.

If I were still teaching new franchise owners, I would still stress a degree of differentiation in the image you wish to create. One of my core beliefs is that appearance counts in dress, speech, message and presentation. The better the package, the better the message is received.

I wish I could claim some special wisdom caused me to use the approach of differentiation, but the truth is it came from my lack of confidence in head-to-head confrontation. Every time I could find a different way to perform a task or present an offer based on something different, it created a higher level of interest in the prospect or client and many times caused him or her to give me a chance to prove the value of my different way. That gave me confidence.

The one thing I knew, as I sought to grow my business, was that there were several very good insurance restoration contracting companies in Duval County and surrounding areas. And I knew that all of them had the contractor image and the contractor sales approach.

My fear of becoming one of the crowd, and my desperate need to differentiate in order to make the property insurer representative remember me and the property owner to see me as someone who was there to truly help them, all those things led to the second Paul Davis mantra, "We put your interest above all others including our own." And we backed that up by doing so time after time in a manner both the insurer and the insured could clearly see.

General Services Administration

Golden Crown Builders got a lot of business from the local General Services Administration (GSA) office. I developed a unit price system that covered each phase of ninety percent of the jobs they asked us to bid on, which was installing or moving pre-fab metal panels to create or modify office spaces. The system was designed after the system we used in insurance restoration contracting work, and charged a set unit price for each task outlined in the work orders provided by the GSA personnel. My program set a fixed unit labor and, if necessary, material cost to be paid to each subcontractor performing the work for Golden Crown Builders, Inc.

When Bob took over Golden Crown Builders, Inc. and I started Paul W. Davis Contracting, Inc., I was chosen by the local GSA management to continue to provide the services they needed. It was a very profitable business and I was very appreciative. There are two events that are worth telling.

Paul W. Davis Contracting, Inc. letterhead, estimates and billing were all done on brown and tan paper using brown ink. We also published a short monthly newsletter that we mailed out called "Done Up Brown." In a normal review of the local General Services Administration operations, the inspector took notice of the amount of brown paper in the office files. This gave cause for the inspector to call for a full review of the local operations.

Bob and I always gave the GSA general manager and the assistant general manager either a ham or a turkey each Christmas. My friend and Sunday school class member—who was the assistant general manager—called me to tell me about the inspection and that I would be contacted. And, that I would be asked if I had ever given any gifts to him or his boss.

I felt a fear like none I had ever felt before. I knew that I had to tell the truth because of my Christian beliefs and also because I would be severely punished if I lied under oath. I tried and tried to come up with a solution, but made no progress.

Sure enough, one morning my secretary called me to say, "There's a man from the FBI who would like to speak to you." My inner response was utter terror. My actual response was, "Please send him in."

The young man who came into my office looked the part he played in law enforcement, which did not calm my fears. After a few minutes of polite conversation, he said that he needed to ask me some questions and that he would need to put me under oath to do so. That raised the fear level another notch. It was like his questions were a ratchet wrench and every time he spoke it tightened the nut a little more. Having sworn me in, he looked straight into my face and asked me, "Mr. Davis, has there ever been any exchange of gifts between you and the local General Services Administration management?"

My understanding of exchange is that of gifts going in both directions. Neither of the men had ever given me a gift of any nature. I could honestly say, "No sir, there has never been any exchange of gifts between me and the local General Services Administration management personnel." He smiled and said, "That's what I needed to hear." We shook hands and he left. I still to this day believe that he worded his question in a manner that would allow me to tell the truth and allow the local GSA managers to escape a very difficult situation. And, to this day I still believe it was a "God thing" that led him to phrase the question in such a manner that a truthful answer would not harm the GSA managers, whose jobs were at stake.

I continued to do work for the General Services Administration and the tasks began to be much larger than they originally were, and many originated from the Atlanta regional office. Eventually the GSA regional management asked me to come to Atlanta and teach their people how to use my program so they could then implement it nationally. I agreed and spent some time in Atlanta teaching the key personnel how our system worked. My understanding was that they used our program in all of their regions. It was the first time that Paul Davis Systems had an operational impact on a national program. But it was not the last.

Division of the Dollar

There are three approaches to success:

- doing the same things everyone else is doing better, which everyone claims to do
- doing it cheaper, thereby reducing your profit and probably the quality of your product
- finding a way to do it differently to obtain a better result, with no price increase

  The goal was to increase profit without increasing pricing.

My experience was that I could accomplish all of the above through the simple program God gave me that I referred to as the "Division of the Dollar." It was simple. Each tradesperson was responsible for the labor and materials to accomplish their particular task and received a set, fair percentage of the selling price for their trade or position as full compensation for themselves and any additional help required.

Our core strategy, developed over a period of time, was to price at the lowest practical price for all parties—insurer, property owner, subcontractors, estimator/salesperson, job supervisor, CEO and stockholders. Each of the above, with the exception of the property owner, insurer and stockholders, received a set percentage of the selling price for their particular trade for which they furnished all labor, transportation and materials.

What it boiled down to is that every person involved in the restoration of the damaged property was paid only for production and never for attendance.

We never had trouble finding people to fill any of the necessary positions. A part of the incentive was that you could earn a very good income by doing good work, not wasting materials, and properly supervising the work of those you might need for the larger jobs.

This was unique in its time and it was based on the company's value system and culture.

We defined value system as what we believed to be true and honest. We defined culture as how we lived out our value system.

Back to Bob

But I need to get back to Bob Schroeder and what happened in his life, which neither of us could have anticipated when we decided to go our separate ways. Soon after the split, Bob became ill and was not able to manage the Golden Crown business.

He had an assistant, but the assistant did not have the confidence of the adjuster Bob did most of his business with. When the adjuster couldn't work with Bob because of the illness, he called and asked if he could work with me. I agreed to make estimates for him but not for Paul W. Davis Contracting, Inc. He agreed that I would make the estimate and if the property owner wanted the work done, we would get the authorization and give the estimate to Bob's assistant, who was my brother Charles, to get the work done. And all of the profit went to Golden Crown Builders, Inc.

There were also some loans that Bob and I both signed for. When the lenders sought to have the loans paid, Golden Crown Builders, Inc., given Bob's physical condition, could not pay them. To keep from ruining Golden Crown Builders' credit, I paid the loans.

As I mentioned before, Bob was a marine sergeant in the Pacific battle with Japan. And rightly so, he carried a lot of pride for that service. I respected him greatly for his service to our country, and I let that respect override any ill-feelings I bore him for our acrimonious split. That dynamic wasn't a good one; the more I did out of friendship and respect, the more anger it caused in Bob. The idea of being dependent on someone else was too much for him to bear gracefully. My respect for him did not waiver.

We didn't speak for several years, then one day out of the blue, my secretary buzzed me and said, "There is a Mr. Bob Schroeder out here who wants to see you."

I was shocked and truthfully a little apprehensive, but I responded, "Send him in."

Bob came in and, not knowing what to expect, I shook hands with him and asked him to sit down.

Lord knows how many years back that this occurred, but I feel close to tears as I write this. After some polite conversation, Bob got to his reason for being there and said something to this effect:

"Paul, when we split up, you did so many good things for me, never asking anything from me in return. And the more you did, the angrier I became.

"But last week, my doctor told me that my heart is in bad shape and that none of the things he's tried have done any good. And that there's nothing more he can do. He suggested that I do whatever is necessary to be best prepared for death.

"I could not die without first coming to you to ask your forgiveness for the way I've treated you, when all you were trying to do was to help me when I could not help myself.

"Will you forgive me?"

By then we were both in tears. We got up and hugged each other for some time. God allowed me to acknowledge all Bob had taught me that had made it possible for me to be where I was at that point. And it gave me great joy that I could say without reservation, "I forgive you and I love you."

After many tears, a lot of good words and a crushing hug, Bob left my office and walked out the door, a man free of all his anger.

Bob died a few weeks later. But my time with him, and that day in particular, was a watershed event in my life. Even as I read this now, my eyes tear up when I think of my relationship and memories of Bob Schroeder.

Chapter 6

FROM PAUL W. DAVIS CONTRACTING TO PAUL W. DAVIS SYSTEMS, INC.

Starting in the Corner Office

When I first started Paul Davis Contracting, it was in an office built in a corner of Mr. Newton's building supply company warehouse. Not expecting much business, I was prepared to do most of the office work myself with part-time help from my wife. When the first month produced $22,000 in sales rather than the $1,200 anticipated, all of this changed.

Erma Nesmith, who became a very loyal employee, agreed to serve as my receptionist and job cost accountant. When I hired her I said, "Bring a book because there may be times when just you are here and have nothing to do." She did, and a few years later she showed me the book and said, "I brought the book, but I have never had time to read a single page."

To a Building of Our Own, or House-Flipping Lesson Learned

In 1967, my brother Charlie Davis brought his marketing expertise to the team and began a working relationship that lasted with very few interruptions until his retirement in 1989. Charlie contributed greatly to the success of Paul Davis Systems.

The beginning of this expansion and the personnel required to allow it to continue created the need for a compensation plan for associates. After we tried many unsuccessful plans, we put one into place that completed the third and fourth fixed points of the Paul Davis Systems plan of operation. These points—which were a fixed cost of sales and a guaranteed gross profit on each job—completed the basic structure of the operational system.

That year we moved from our warehouse location to an office above a small job printing company in a converted garage apartment on the corner of St. Augustine Road and Sheridan Street. The property was purchased from Erma Nesmith, and while operations continued at that location through 1984, it didn't take us long to realize we'd outgrown the second floor garage apartment.

We built a new office behind the garage apartment. It was a proud day when we moved in. Then we had to get rid of the garage apartment. I called a wrecking company that wanted $3,000 to do the job. Before I agreed, a man came by and asked if I wanted to tear it down and get it off the lot. He agreed to do the job for $1,000. I could save $2,000, and agreed to give him the job only if he understood he would not be paid until the lot was completely clear.

A few days later I drove up to find a house-moving company jacking up the second floor and demolishing the bottom. When I asked what they were doing they said they had bought the house for $2,000 from the man I had agreed to pay $1,000. When I asked them what they were going to do with the house, they said they were moving it down the street to the man who'd paid them $5,000 for it—lesson one for me and my lack of management skills. It didn't show good business sense on my part, but the fun that I have had telling that story over the years has made the cost more than worthwhile.

Write It Down

Before we opened the first branch office in Orlando in 1968, we had already developed a pretty good system for every part of the operations. Bill Richardson introduced me to a couple who were his close friends. When they understood what he was doing, they asked about opening another branch office in Gainesville, Florida. I finally realized that there was a vast difference in having a system in your mind and having a system on paper, which can be taught and sent away with the pupil.

I got my secretary to get me one of those little recording things you could hold in your hand and record your thoughts, even if you were driving. And then later someone could listen to it and transfer the message to paper (in my day, which was many years back, that was state-of-the-art technology). I used the recorder going to and coming from Orlando, and my secretary typed it week by week. It became the first written operations manual for what became Paul W. Davis Systems Operation Manual. It was small, but it was a manual.

The Five-Point Star

The basic structure of Paul W. Davis Contracting, and then Paul Davis Systems and later Paul Davis Franchising, was a fixed selling price and a fixed cost.

The objective was to fix the cost per unit for each of the five basic functions based on the quantity of each function on any particular job.

Each function was allotted a set percentage of the income derived from that function on each job sold to cover the cost of that function. What this enabled management to do was to know, even before the work was begun, the amount of profit to be earned on that particular job.

The purpose of the five-point star was to simplify the management by naming five basic points to continually manage.

The Five-Point PD Management Star

Fixed selling price

Low overhead   Fixed cost of sales

Guaranteed gross profit   Fixed production cost

The Start of Franchising

Earl Sandifer and his wife were very committed Christians who worked as missionaries to France. They came home for furlough every two years, and it was on one of these breaks that Earl learned about my success in creating branch offices. A short time after that he was visiting a church in Louisville, Kentucky, where he met a member who was a franchise salesman for The Captain's Table restaurant chain. Earl talked with him about what I was doing and the salesman said, "tell him that he should consider franchising his program." When Earl returned, he told me about that conversation.

Franchising was a lot newer and far less accepted in those days, and my first reaction to Earl's suggestion was to laugh. However, the more I thought about the idea, the more it appealed to me.

I had a general idea about franchises, having bought two that ultimately failed. But I had very little grasp as to the role of the franchisor. I talked with my attorney and he gave me an outline of what a franchise agreement would look like. I created a rough draft and the attorney polished it up. It was a standard agreement in all aspects except one. The one major difference was that the agreement created a Paul Davis Systems council through which the franchisee contributed to the operational system with the franchisor. It is on that unique principle that the organization has built its strength and realized so much success.

The first franchise was in Tampa, Florida, and was purchased by Don Goldberg and his church minister. Don was a estimator/salesman in the Jacksonville office. I went to Tampa once a week for several months, and then as the need arose, to help him establish one of the most successful franchises of the early years.

My brother Bill was living in the north and wanted to come south to restart his life. He came down to spend a few days fishing at a camp where I went every year. We talked about him running the Orlando branch office and eventually converting it to a franchise. Bill was a good negotiator and I would have done anything to get him and his family back in Florida. We reached an agreement, we signed after our return, and a short time later he and Marty moved to Orlando. Bill made a success out of his franchise; eventually he sold it for a considerable sum, and continued living in Florida until his death.

The first franchise was established in 1969, and the rest, as they say, is history.

Bill Horn's Franchise, or, The Lengths We'll Go to for Our Franchisees

Bill Horn is and always has been as close as anyone could come to being the ideal franchise owner-operator. He'd heard about Paul Davis Systems, Inc. from his cousin who owned the franchise in West Palm Beach. Hearing what his cousin was doing and given that Bill was looking for a job, he called me and after our conversation I promised to come and talk with him and meet his wife, Frankie. I went the next day. Bill met me at the airport and we drove to his house where, once they got a grasp of what Paul Davis Systems was, they agreed they wanted to buy a franchise. I told them the price was $20,000, and he asked if they could give me $10,000 then and the balance when he came to Jacksonville for training. I agreed, went back to Jacksonville, and he followed a few weeks later. Back then, training was spending time with me and doing all the things he would be required to do in his franchise, which is a far cry from the sophisticated training process that is in place today.

A few days after he finished his training and had returned to Louisville to start calling on adjusters, he called to tell me that a private plane from Jacksonville had crashed into the back of a home and the adjuster asked him to prepare an estimate and, if the property owners agreed, to begin the repairs.

I asked him to meet me at the airport the next day and we had the estimate completed before the end of the day. The claims manager, whom we met with the next day, was well pleased with Bill's estimate. In the conversation, the claims manager said that he'd first called the contractor who was doing most of his restoration work. The contractor didn't return the call, so, recognizing the need to get started, he remembered Bill calling on him and contacted him.

It was a fantastic start and Bill never missed a beat as he grew to be the most successful franchisee of that time.

Of course, I always claimed that I sent that plane to show just how much support we provide to new franchisees.

Defining the Culture and Value System

Every business has a value system and every business has a culture. These two, whether you understand them or not, drive your business. For any organization to enjoy the greatest potential for success, its culture must always reflect its basic values.

We adhere to the truth, "There is Strength in Unity." Although we are proud of our individual ownership, we are equally proud of and dedicated to the concept of oneness as an organization.

We feel strongly that while the entire organization should care for each individual member, the well-being of the organization transcends that of any single member.

We recognize that, of all the parties in our marketplace, none is so important as the property insurance industry and its individual field claims personnel and management. We will conduct our business in such a way as to be an invaluable asset to them in their efforts to settle property losses. To accomplish this, we commit ourselves without reservation to the following pledge:

We will approach every task you assign us with absolute honesty and integrity.

We will put your interest above all others including our own.

Our purpose in preparing an appraisal will always be to arrive at the lowest equitable price the adjuster and property owner can use to settle the claim.

We will never misrepresent the scope or cause of loss in order to obtain an authorization to make repairs.

We will provide any service you need at no cost, having proved over the years that sales are a natural by-product of our service.

We believe and practice the old Rotary motto: "He profits most who serves the best."

We acknowledge the four prerequisites to fulfilling this pledge are:

- Total honesty and integrity in all relationships.
- Professionalism in every aspect of business.
- Sound business management and accountability through adherence to the Paul Davis Restoration operational system.
- Commitment to continuing industry-related education.

The Computer Program

Probably the biggest event in the history of Paul Davis Systems was the design and implementation of computer-driven insurance restoration estimating and job-costing systems.

An adjuster called me one day in 1981, to say that a company was coming to demonstrate a computer system designed to be used by insurance adjusters; he asked if I would like to attend. Of course, I said yes and for the first time saw a program specifically designed for insurance adjusters.

I came back to the office convinced that this could be another first for Paul Davis Systems. I found a store that sold computers and went to see what they cost. They were expensive and did not include programming, whatever that meant. The store owner gave me Frank Novak's name and phone number. I called Frank and he came to the office to see our operation and determine whether or not he could help us.

He could and he did and has always been one of my heroes. Frank said he would need a detailed step-by-step list of the various processes. It was music to my ears. I filled nineteen pages of a legal pad with our processes and gave them to him.

He then created the first insurance restoration estimating system.

Later I did another nineteen pages of step-by-step notes from which he created the first insurance restoration job-costing system.

Canada

One day in 1986, our receptionist buzzed me and said, "You have a call from Canada. Do you want to take it?" I said, "Yes, put it through."

The callers introduced themselves as Bill Robinson and Ken Robinson, father and son. They had seen an advertisement about a new company in the U.S. and wanted to learn more about it. I welcomed the opportunity and began to explain what Paul W. Davis Systems, Inc. was all about. They listened and asked questions for about fifteen minutes, and agreed that it sounded like a good opportunity. (It was not until sometime afterward that they admitted they thought we were an insurance agency and that was why they called.) They seemed very interested but they were not contractors, which they did not realize was a requirement.

We had a training program for new franchisees planned in two weeks. I suggested that if they were interested they could attend that class without making a commitment. They came, they found it to be a good opportunity and they returned to Canada. We set a date for me to come to Canada to work out the details, make some sales calls and to recruit the first subcontractors.

We later agreed that they would become the Canadian franchisor. The rest is more history.

Brenda Enters

When Brenda came onto the scene, I am sure she had no idea what she was getting herself into. In 1989, my business life was doing really well—I was attending meetings of The Executive Committee, the business was growing, we were searching for a chief operating officer to allow me the freedom to develop more programs—but my personal life was an absolute mess.

I was divorced. I had ceased attending church. I had been betrayed by a franchise owner without cause. I was drinking far more than I should have been.

Brenda Staver moved to Jacksonville to become a consultant to my company in July. Her position as part of the business was purely professional, and had nothing to do with my personal life. But once she was in Jacksonville our friendship took hold and began to grow. Over time, we became closer and our relationship became more personal and less centered on business. She convinced me to listen to a lot of Christian music. My way back turned out to be one of the most difficult periods of my personal and business life.

The personal price Brenda paid in order to lead me back to Christianity was high. She influenced me to change my drinking, my language and my personal health. She also inherited the issue of my two younger children from my second marriage. They were totally out of control at that point. No man could ask for better children than they are today as grownups. I think if you were to ask them they would agree that Brenda had a huge influence on their lives.

I had known Brenda for many, many years before she moved to Jacksonville as a member of our very large extended family. I had always admired and loved her as a member of the family. She never made a big fuss about the status of my personal life at any given moment, which was a good thing. Over time I found myself loving her as a person as opposed to just a member of the family. I knew that I had placed myself at risk as a person and I needed what she was willing to give.

As I slowly returned to what for me was the normal life, we decided we should marry and enjoy each other full-time. I can truthfully say that no business decision I have ever made could even come close to being as rewarding as Brenda's agreement to marry me. We married in December of 1989. She is still the center of my life now in 2016, and is always there when I need her. As I write this at the age of eighty-eight, our relationship is just as solid as a relationship can be. She is still my "Sweet Brenda."

Gold Mining, or, While Most Contractors want Big Jobs, PDS Built Its Record on the Small Ones

Brenda and I had the pleasure of touring Alaska. The one thing that stood out to me, other than the boredom of hours on the bus, was a visit to a gold mine. The old dredge was still there and our guide explained how it worked.

This operation was quite a ways away from the romantic picture we so often have of the solitary prospector, working the creeks alone, seeking nuggets of gold at the water's edge. This was a huge commercial vessel that could be moved in any direction by cables on the front, back and sides.

It scooped up mud from the bottom of the creek using a large crane that then deposited the load in the bucket on the dredge. It drew the mud into a long sluice ending at the rear of the dredge. The slanted sluice had crossbars in its bottom located at specific intervals. The gold dust and the small nuggets would settle there to be gathered and melted into bars of gold, which would become the source of income for the owner.

The most amazing thing to me was that the dredge owner and operators knew that the large nuggets would pass through the sluice to be thrown out at the end. As I heard this from our guides, I was amazed that except in rare cases, the big nuggets (of which there were few) were considered of less, if any, value by these commercial prospectors.

This made me think of one of the Paul Davis Systems mantras: "We are willing to do your big jobs if you will give us your small jobs."

This was a fine example of how the Paul Davis Systems mindset was the complete opposite to that of the vast majority of insurance restoration contractors. Their approach was "we are willing to do your small jobs if you will give us your big jobs as well."

To me, Paul Davis Systems franchisees and the franchisor were the dredge. The cables that moved us were the insurance agents, the insurers' regional and corporate property claims departments, the property owners who experienced the covered loss, and our franchisees.

It was the continuing tug of the needs of each of these that enabled the franchisor to move as necessary to be in the optimum partnership position to serve and profit from all the needs of each of these clients.

It is the illustration of a mantra, "At Paul Davis Systems, Inc. everything is cast in putty." This was true of everything at Paul Davis Systems, Inc. except for our culture and our value system.

It was from this cast-in-putty mindset that we developed the key principles by which we conducted our business. Our primary mantra was "Paul Davis Systems is not about doing things better, Paul Davis Systems is about doing things differently to obtain a better result."

Did that small-job mentality work out for us? Absolutely! When the business was sold in 1997, the franchisees performed approximately $240,000,000 of repairs that year, and the average size job was less than $3,500.

Most insurance restoration contractors would see that as a failure to capture the market. Paul Davis Systems took the opposite approach. Let the sluice capture the dust and let the big nuggets fall where they may.

The franchisees who followed all five points of the Paul Davis system averaged a profit of ten to fourteen percent. And that was after paying the owner/manager five percent of all sales as his or her compensation as the manager. I doubt that any honest, independent insurance restoration contractor did anywhere near as well.

No one who has benefited from ownership in the Paul Davis Systems franchise network had anything to do with its creation. That evolved from a series of events that sometimes were exciting and joyful but at other times were tense and unpleasant.

But literally thousands of people, including insurers, adjusters, property owners, franchise owners and their contract service providers and subcontractors are a part of what we became and profited from their participation.

The entire network thrived on the "dust," with a few nuggets thrown in from time to time.

Betrayal: The Heart Breaker

I have been betrayed in business three times. I was and probably still am an easy target for those who use guile or deceit to accomplish their goals in business or in life in general. I think I can, without offense, say that my openness and vulnerability are the result of my mother's influence living in me, even now at age eighty-eight.

Sometimes we may be guilty of betraying someone who has done absolutely nothing to deserve the betrayal. Such was the case of my betrayal of my wife Loyce more than forty years ago. Loyce was dying of Schilder Diffuse Sclerosis, an extremely rare illness with only nine cases documented since it was discovered in 1912. Even as I write this, I feel the shame and disgrace of my indiscretion. That led to my second marriage and two wonderful children, Emily and Paul Jr.

It was more than ten years after Loyce's death that Brenda came into my life and began the process of bringing me back into fellowship with God. Brenda became my third wife and we have been happily married some twenty-six years.

I have been betrayed three times in my business career, and twice by the same person. The first instance came early in my building of the franchise program. I was excited about our program—we had seven franchises over three states—and wanted to have a group meeting to discuss proposed programs and get the approval of the franchisees.

As I was preparing for the meeting, I learned that a trusted employee was telling our franchisees that they should always come to him with their concerns because he knew more about their needs than I did. I told him that I was going to let him go, but gave him six months' notice so he could find a new job. (Did I mention dumb?) He sat in on all planning sessions for the upcoming meeting and my goals for it.

Without my knowledge, he called the franchisees and told them that I was out to control them and to reduce their profitability. His objective was two-fold: first, to punish me, and second, to take over all of the franchise operations and continue the program in his own name.

Prior to the group meeting I gave my people instructions to get as close as possible to each of the franchise owners, make sure they had copies of the agenda and to assure them that our purpose was to help them with any problems they were facing.

The next morning we assembled, and after a short period of socializing I moved to the platform and called the meeting to order. I launched into my proposal of programs that I thought would help us to grow in numbers and increase each franchisee's volume of sales. As I stood and spoke, I looked out over the group and was shocked to see absolutely no response to a presentation that I thought would have been well received. When I finished there was still no response, just the same blank look as they stood and walked out without a word to me.

After they were gone, my people and I met to talk about what had happened. One person said that just before the meeting, my terminated employee had contacted all of the franchisees to tell them that I had instructed my employees to spy on them to find out what they were thinking. And that my whole purpose for the meeting was to find ways to punish franchisees who did not do what they were told.

I truly lost all self-control. I ranted and raved about the betrayal of that employee. Afterward, I came back to Jacksonville and made arrangements to go to a South Florida resort to sort out my feelings. Bill Horn, who was fairly new to the group, recognizing that I was deeply hurt, agreed to come down and spend some time with me. In retrospect, he was a lifesaver, because he listened as I ranted and raved, using horrible words and all sorts of threats of revenge.

After four days, even Bill had reached his limit of endurance and returned home to Kentucky. But he had brought me to the point that I could at least begin to think about solutions rather than revenge. As a result, I began to think more clearly. I knew that if I was going to salvage the franchise program, I had to regain the respect of the franchise owners and assure them that I understood that my success rested on their success.

When I returned to Jacksonville, my anger was gone. I put that part of my life behind me, determined to focus on the present and the future. I believed then and still believe today that God was using those events to direct my path into the new programs that He put in my mind, which made us a cohesive group rather than adversaries.

Over a very short period of time I visited each franchisee and brought them into the process of restructuring our business relationships.

I designed a dispute resolution process that used franchisees and the franchisor to determine the outcome.

I designed a security fund, in which every franchise was required to build, over time, a deposit of $9,000. The purpose was to assure insurers and their adjusters that any problems on any job would, in the event of a failure of any franchise, be properly completed without risk to the property owner or insurer.

The wife of one of the franchisees distrusted everything and created constant turmoil in the franchise group. I followed the advice of Congressman Sam Rayburn of Texas, who said, "Hug your friends, but hug your enemies even tighter." I made certain that she knew and understood the purpose of each change I recommended.

I contacted the franchise owners and got their agreement to have another franchisee meeting in Tampa, Florida. I believe that no franchise organization before Paul Davis had ever become a democratic program the way we did. We had a good turnout and the mood seemed to be very positive. It was also the first formal event that the soon-to-be franchisee from Canada and his son attended. We presented the new programs and discussed one at a time. The only program that received any resistance was the security fund, the one requiring that each franchise contribute $9,000.

A time was set for a second meeting to finalize the changes. All went well and everything was approved with minor changes. Necessary committees were formed and a president and vice president were elected for the franchise council. In retrospect, I can see God's hand there: "And we know that all things work together for good to them that love God, to them who are the called according to His purpose" (Romans 8:28, KJV).

The Wage and Hour Visit

One day after Paul W. Davis Systems, Inc. had been successful with its subcontracting program, my receptionist called me and said, "There are two gentlemen here from the Wage and Hour office who want to talk with you."

They were very nice and explained that they were there to be sure I was paying the proper percentage of Social Security on my employee wages.

I listened and answered, "I understand but we don't have any employees. All of our people are subcontractors and do not get salaries."

Their response was, "That's good but would you mind letting us see your contracts?" to which I replied, "We don't have any contracts. We just trust each other to be fair."

They responded, "Mr. Davis, we can only recognize them as subcontractors if they have a contract with your company. We'll work with your accountant and let you know where you stand."

The subcontractors loved it because they already made more money than they had before, and now they were about to receive a bonus. Not only were we responsible to pay the Social Security, but each subcontractor had to guess at the number of hours they worked in excess of eight hours a day, and we had to pay time and a half of estimated hours. The total in taxes and salaries came to something over $10,000, which was equal to $20,000 or more in today's economy.

I went to see my attorney and we began the process of creating contracts for all subcontracted work. He gave me a copy of the twelve requirements used to classify whether workers are independent contractors or regular employees.

After that, whenever the Wage and Hour people found one of our franchisees operating in their territory, they immediately went to their office for an audit. I instructed all franchisees that if this happened to them they were to ask to have the audit at a time when I could be present. Using the twelve requirements the Wage and Hour Division had set, and using our subcontractor contracts, it took very little time to verify the subcontractor status of our program. After a few years, and losing every audit, the Wage and Hour people gave up.

Some Paul Davis Systems Firsts, and Some Wisdom from My Momma

We had many firsts at PDS. Here are just a few:

The first, open-to-insurers, printed price lists.

The first fixed selling price / fixed production cost program.

The first printed one-year warranty to property owners and insurers.

The first funded, independent corporation to insure our guarantees.

The first computer-generated estimates.

The first computer-generated job-cost tracking program.

The first international insurance restoration contracting services.

The first franchise program where the franchisor and the franchisees contributed to the operational system.

The first franchisee / franchisor dispute resolution program.

The first published value system and culture statement that defines the Paul Davis Systems standard.

The first contractor services–insurer home office relationship.

In the midst of all of this was the old Paul, who dreamed of but never expected to see all of the remarkable things that were happening. And the old Paul never ceased to tell anyone who would listen all about it. When I was feeling pretty satisfied with my success, I would often go back in my mind to one Sunday, when Loyce and I had gone to my mother's for dinner. My mother said, "Paul, let's go out and sit on the front porch for a while." I agreed and we did. I am not sure exactly what we were talking about, but given that period of my life, I feel sure it was me talking about me. After a while, Momma said, "Paul, do you remember that terrible inferiority complex you had?" I answered, "Yes Momma, it was so hurtful." Her response was, "Paul, you could sure use some of it now." I am sure it didn't cure my inflated ego, but she sure put it in a way that was not as offensive as it could have been.

Our Silver Anniversary

The silver anniversary of Paul Davis Systems was in 1991. What began as two simple objectives designed to provide a living for one family has grown tremendously. Twenty-five years in that operating plan consisted of more than seventy-five integrated business systems used by more than 150 franchise owners throughout the United

States and Canada, with an equal number of associates and an equal number of job cost accountants. Given the total organization plus countless tradesmen and their employees, several thousand families derived their incomes from what twenty-five years before then was not even a dream.

The United Services Automobile Association (USAA) Visit

One morning, well after the beginning of franchising, I was told that a gentleman from USAA Insurance Company would like to speak to me. He came in and I asked Brenda to come in as well. He said that his home office had heard a lot about Paul Davis Systems through our contact with their Tampa, Florida, regional office and that the purpose of his visit was to learn as much as possible about our company.

As soon as I was able to get back to Earth, we discussed our systems and demonstrated our computer programs, which were the only insurance restoration contracting business programs in existence at that time. He was very impressed and asked me to come to their home office in Texas.

I agreed, and we set a date. The visit was made and a lot was learned by both parties. Over a short period of time, I made several visits to meet with and talk to a number of their people. I explained our program to a meeting of all their regional property loss general managers. Later, I met with other executives to discuss a plan that would use Paul Davis Systems for all property claims in the south central office that required a contractor.

When I met with the Texas franchisees who were to be in the pilot program, the same woman who spearheaded the original rebellion at the first ever General Council meeting heard about it in her franchise office. She took it upon herself to protect the franchisees who were to be in the pilot program against non-franchisee contractors using our program.

I will spare you the details of what I saw as her seeking revenge for having lost the position of being the key woman in our system.

At the end of the day she won this battle, and I was forced to turn the program over to a company employee who would leave the company to build the organization USAA wanted, and become wealthy doing so. His commitment, in exchange for the right to take over the program, was that if he was successful he would pay Paul Davis Systems $240,000 for the rights to the program. He could not have done so without my releasing him from his non-compete agreement. He has become very successful, but he has never paid a penny of the agreed amount.

From the franchisee side, a large adjusting company, seeing the success of the USAA program, started a national program furnishing contractor services to property insurers. Any Paul Davis Systems franchisee who does not want to lose the business they were getting directly from property insurers has to join the new program and kick-back three and one-half percent of all jobs they receive from this company. That is in addition to the three and one-half percent they pay to the franchisor.

I don't think the lady who successfully stopped Paul Davis Systems from providing what USAA asked for is seen as much of a heroine throughout the franchise organization today.

Moving on

From my personal standpoint, I am sad to admit that the ending to the whole United Services Automobile Association experience broke my spirit and over a short period of time led to my selling a business I loved. In retrospect, I can see how by letting a woman and three men, all franchisees, get in my head, I failed to use all the protection I had designed into the franchise council program.

All of that is the downside; the upside is that, having sold the company, I could begin to reestablish and renew my commitment and enjoyment of "the peace of God, that passeth all understanding," (Philippians 4:7, KJV). My salvation was intact since the single, lifetime event that established it years ago. I could also help others. As a gift of the Holy Spirit, I am able by word and deed to counsel and help individuals who are hurting, who need to establish or re-establish their relationship with God, and to enjoy the peace and joy of that relationship.

Chapter 7
SOME PEOPLE WHO HAVE INFLUENCED MY LIFE

My Mother

My Momma, Mary Susan Woodall Davis (1889-1971) had the most direct influence on my life and gave me the foundation on which my future was built. She was a quiet, committed person who accepted life as it was, at any given moment, and by the choice of her will, made the best of it.

She lost her first son at the age of nine months of what was then referred to as "crib death." Her second child was also a boy, who also died tragically at the age of nine months, again of crib death. I remember hearing her say that one of the most difficult times of her life was when her third child, Joe, was nine months old. She would wake and look into the crib with fear. But God was gracious and Joe thrived, and starting as a boot, over the years became a captain in the U.S. Navy. She bore and raised five sons, two by her first husband who died and three by her second husband, who was my father.

I think of the five, my brother Bob and I were the most like my mother in our outlook and our response to life.

My Father

My father, Daddy, Charles C. Davis, Sr. (1884-1981) was a good man. He was born in southern Georgia, one of six children. He was a small man, thin and about five feet tall. He worked hard and he walked fast. I never heard him use a curse word. He used terms such as "aw shaw" when he was frustrated, or "I'll be John C W twisted" when surprised, or the ultimate "Methuselah, grindstones and hoe handles."

I never met his father, who was an itinerant preacher. But his mother lived her last years with us. She was not a doting grandmother, but rather, she had high expectations of her grandchildren in terms of the services she felt she was due. Accordingly, we treated her very well. She died at age ninety-six. People on my dad's side of the family, for the most part, lived long lives. He died at ninety-seven, a brother lived to ninety-three, and a sister lived to 103.

My dad worked for Independent Life Insurance Company as a debit collector. His territory covered the rural part of Duval County south of the St. Johns River, the Jacksonville Beaches and the Fernandina area west of the St. Marys River. He collected monthly premiums from his policyholders that ran from ten cents up to a dollar.

He worked five-and-a-half days a week and furnished his own car, gas and upkeep. His average weekly earnings were $19. That might not seem like much income, but to put it in perspective, gas was ten cents a gallon, bread was ten cents a loaf and the payment on his home was eight dollars per month.

During World War II, he and my mother converted our garage into a laundry business. They had an electric washing machine, which Daddy operated, and a large electric ironing machine, which was Momma's assignment. After the war ended, more and more people bought their own washers and dryers and my parents had to close the laundry business.

Momma went to work at Cohen's department store, which was a very impressive store in its day. Daddy was hired by our church to maintain the church and grounds, a task he undertook with his usual total commitment. As they grew older, my parents had to give up their jobs and live on Social Security, which was net $45, plus some help from their five boys.

Momma died at eighty-two and Daddy passed away at ninety-seven.

Joseph "Joe" Daniel Jeffords

My eldest half-brother Joe (1912-1980) was born in Lake Wales, Florida, to my mother and her first husband. He was her third son after her first- and second-born sons died of crib death.

Joe was raised in difficult times but finished high school. My mother knew a member of the U.S. House of Representatives and asked him if he would use his influence to get Joe a position as a navy recruit. It was not an easy task in those days. He agreed and did get Joe a position as a recruit in the U.S. Navy. By the time the U.S. declared war in WW II, Joe had worked his way up to senior warrant officer, the highest position for the non-commissioned. He was then promoted to ensign, a commissioned officer.

Joe never talked much about the war, but he had far more battle experience than the other four of us put together. He never displayed his medals, but they were many. He retired not too long before his death.

Robert "Bob" Gilbert Jeffords

Bob (1917-1984) was Momma's fourth son with her first husband, and the younger of my two half-brothers. He was truly a remarkable man in every sense of the word. Of all the people I have ever known, he came nearest to being a true and consistent Christian in every sense of the word.

Bob fell in love with a classmate, Sally Newton, and married her after graduation. Mr. Newton, Sally's father, worked for Mason Lumber Company. He also had a very close relationship with the manager of the Jacksonville office of the National Biscuit Company (Nabisco). He asked the manager if he would get Bob a job. He hired Bob at Nabisco, which turned out to be the only employer Bob had in his entire career.

Bob began as a janitor in the warehouse, but he did the job well and over time worked his way up the business ladder to serve as assistant to the national president of Nabisco. He was given a branch to manage and did the job so well that his last years were spent moving from branch to branch to help them to overcome problems and become more productive.

Ever resourceful, during the height of the Depression, Bob would somehow get drums of cookies past their time limit sent to our house to feed the hogs. Truth be known, my friends and I ate the best of them before the hogs got their share.

Bob was a mentor to me as a high school dropout and he helped me to get my first real job after I was discharged from the army at the end of the war. Of all the members of our family, Bob was by far the most practical and caring of my brothers. Bob had a powerful and meaningful impact on my life in general and on my business and Christian life in particular.

Mary Davis Staver

Mary (1917-2008) was my half-sister. She was born to my father, Charles C. Davis and his first wife, Ruth. Ruth died while she and Daddy lived in South Georgia, and she had requested that at her death, Mary would go to live with her sister, Mary's Aunt None. She lived there until she graduated from high school, at which time she moved to Miami to marry Robert "Bob" L. Staver, Sr. She ended up living in Jacksonville and was a member of the Glendale Community Church, and died at the age of ninety.

Charles Cleveland Davis, Jr.

Charlie (1922-2006) was married to Yvonne for 55 years, and they are survived by four children, all of whom are living with fond memories of their father.

He was as poor a school student as I was and he left school in the tenth grade. He worked locally for some time and then moved to Savannah, Georgia, for work. While he was there, the U.S. entered the war as a result of the Pearl Harbor bombing. Charlie volunteered for service but was found to have a leaking heart valve and was rejected. So he joined the merchant marine as a wiper working below deck in the engine room. Charlie said he had a very difficult time finding a third ship that would take him because of his record: the first one was torpedoed and sunk; the second was caught in a hurricane and crashed into the rocks off the coast of Scotland.

Charlie was also a great help to me in the later years when I needed help to get the new franchisees started. Very few people could then or even now understand what an important role Charlie played in those early days.

William Bernard Davis

Bill (1923-early 2000) was the middle child of us three Davis boys: he was very intelligent and quick to respond to any wrongdoing. Bill was far more like Daddy, Charlie like Momma, and I am a mixture of both.

Bill, like Joe and Bob, finished high school. In his last year, the U.S. became a part of the battle for freedom of all people, all over the globe. Bill signed up for the air force. After his final training he was shipped to the Pacific theatre. His squadron was assigned to attack the enemy from the air with bombs and machine guns, opening the way so the marines could move in and conquer more and more of the enemy-held territory. He also served as a pilot in the Korean War, making night attacks.

I asked Bill after the war if he had seen any enemy planes. He answered, "I did once but one of us flew behind a cloud and I still can't remember which" (you realize that was a joke).

Bill bought the Orlando, Florida, PDS franchise in the early years and ran it very well. He sold the franchise and retired. He was always busy and one day as he was working on his roof he fell. He died from the fall. I still miss him.

Rev. Robert Ezell

Robert was my cousin and my friend. We were great friends growing up and I still remember many, many fun times we shared. We lived a little over three miles from each other but that did not affect our close relationship. Robert had a bike so he came to my house more than I did his, but we got together, no matter what.

In the summer months, Momma would get extra ice from the ice-man who came one morning each week. She would wrap it in a croker sack and put in under the edge of the house to slow its melting as much as possible. In the afternoon, she would put all the ingredients for homemade ice cream together and we three boys would take turns working the handle of the churn. Robert had a knack for knowing the right days to show up and become a part of the process and especially the enjoyment of eating it.

Robert was a devout Christian (he became a very effective Baptist minister right after the close of World War II). Reverend Witty, a very successful Baptist minister for whom Robert had great respect, was preaching a revival at a church just on the other side of the St. Johns River. Robert convinced me that I should go with him and suggested that he ride his bike and I would ride on the handlebars. We did fine until we reached the St. Johns River Bridge, which was a lift bridge. Obviously Robert could not pedal up the bridge with me on the bars. We walked up the bridge with Robert pushing the bike. At the top we got back on the bike for the ride down.

The bridge ended at the Broad Street viaduct and as I saw the cars going by and became aware of the ninety-degree left turn we would need to make to avoid driving into the traffic, I got scared. As my fear increased so did my stiffness on the bike handlebars, and that made it more and more difficult for Robert to control the bike. We went off the bridge, falling into the traffic. I will always believe that God had his hand on Robert for the ministry and He had to protect me in order to protect Robert. We did get to the revival but I did not become converted at that time. Robert got us home on the slightly damaged bike and we never challenged that bridge again.

Every year Robert and I sold Christmas trees cut out of the top of larger, taller trees. We didn't charge much and so they sold well in those recession days. The average price was 50¢. By now you can guess who did the climbing (I always recognized that I qualified as a devout coward).

As I mentioned, Robert had a bike and I did not. One day as we were riding on what was then Hogan Road, I saw to the side of the road what looked like a package of cigarettes. Robert stopped and I got off the handlebars and got the package. There were four cigarettes missing, but in their place were four one-dollar bills.

We had no idea who the owner might have been so we felt no guilt in keeping them. As we discussed this good fortune, a huge amount in those Depression days, we decided that God had let us find this package, so we would throw the cigarettes away in recognition of God's gift. We both smoked when we could get cigarettes, so we saw this as an act of appreciation. We each kept $2 and we shared expenses as we used the money. And you guessed right if you guessed the majority of the $4 went to buy cigarettes.

Robert joined the navy as soon as his age would permit. He was sent to England and became a part of the Normandy invasion, a major turning point of that war.

He piloted one of the many small landing craft carrying men and supplies to the beachhead landing site. They were all under constant fire by the German army on shore. I still can't begin to imagine what it felt like to be at such horrible risk. After the war, I asked Robert, "Were you scared in the midst of all that?" He said yes, he was very frightened, but he could not betray the men who were in harm's way on those heavily armed enemy beaches.

One of the things I will always remember about Robert occurred after he moved to Orlando. Paul Davis Systems was opening its first office outside of Jacksonville. Robert and I were having lunch and I began to tell him about our moving to franchise our program. I talked about how it would work and I discussed the franchise fee and the royalty payments.

Robert stopped me and asked, "Are you saying these people are going to pay you money for your allowing them to own a business?"

I replied yes, and again, the rest is history.

It was also Robert who helped me to begin the long journey home from the guilt of my betrayal of my first wife, Loyce, a horrible apostate action that still haunts and hurts as I write this today.

Mr. Brack Newton

Mr. Newton was my childhood hero. Not because I really knew him but because I saw him drive past my school bus stop almost every day in his Oldsmobile, which was the biggest car in town, with a cigar in his mouth and the look of the richest man in town. Much of my success evolved from his positive influence on my personal and business life. But, he was also responsible for some of the most difficult periods of my life as well.

And in retrospect, I can see clearly how God used the positive and the negative of my relationship with Mr. Newton to bring me to where I ended up at Paul W. Davis Systems, Inc.

Mr. Torbert

Mr. Torbert was a very shy man who was responsible for the accuracy in the calculations and billing of all sales made by Mason Lumber Company employees.

He was the man assigned with the task of teaching the new kid (me) all the basics of being a Mason Lumber Company employee. He and he alone convinced me that I could fill the position at the sales desk left vacant by an employee who failed to show up for work on a particular Monday morning. He was fired and I started the first job that brought me to my life's career.

Mrs. McEachern

When Loyce and I relocated to Tiger Hole to open Brackridge Paints and Hardware, Bob got us to agree to come to Sunday school at

Glendale Community Church. After a few Sundays, he convinced us to stay for the church service as well. Our Sunday school teacher was Mrs. McEachern. She taught the truth that led to the transformation of my life. And even today, at age eighty-eight, that truth is the core belief that enables me to live as near as possible a tranquil life.

What she lived and consistently taught is the state of living in fellowship with God, and that means having no known unconfessed sin in your life. I was in my early thirties and she was in her late sixties, but she never failed to help by phone or in person as I sought to maintain my fellowship with God.

Professors at Columbia Bible College

I never attended Columbia Bible College, but the school and its professors had a powerful impact on my life in general, and on the single most important decision I made in my entire life. It was a Columbia Bible College professor who spoke that night at Glendale Community Church on the subject of "Seek ye first the Kingdom of God and His righteousness, and all these things shall be added unto you." It became that night, and still is, the mantra by which I seek to live.

Tom Kline

Tom was the property adjuster for Linder & Company, Inc. Insurance Adjusters. He is the man Earl Linder called in at the end of the first meeting Bob Schroeder and I had with him. Tom taught me the basics of insurance restoration contracting, a business I had no idea existed. He also taught me the roles each of the three parties involved—property owner, insurer, contractor—played. He gave me a copy of his one-page price list he used on simple claims, consisting of nine items. Tom was the first of what became a good number of property adjusters who enabled Bob Schroeder and me to build Golden Crown Builders, Inc. But Tom was there at the very beginning, helping lay the foundation that enabled me to come to the place where I can write this history.

An Evangelist at Glendale Community Church

I was often called on to preach in our church and several others. I was a layman and given the fact that God had given me the gift, I was torn between business and the ministry. During my first marriage, Loyce did not want me to go into full-time ministry. One afternoon after an evangelist had spoken, I was standing with him at the front steps. I told him about the conflict I faced concerning the ministry. I asked him for his advice. His response was, "Paul, if God will let you do anything other than preach, don't go into the ministry." I had my answer. God was giving me a measure of success and I decided that was my answer. The feeling of conflict disappeared as I stood there. I went home eager to share this experience with Loyce. She smiled when I finished and said she was grateful. She then said that she had committed to God that day, that if He wanted me in the ministry, she would work to be the best pastor's wife she could be. This increased my belief that God's Holy Spirit lives in every born-again believer: "And we know that all things work together for good to them that love God, to them who are the called according to His purpose" (Romans 8:28, KJV).

Bill Richardson

Bill was truly one of my heroes. I met him when we were both members of the Youth for Christ board of advisors in Jacksonville, Florida. I felt an instant sense of brotherhood the moment we met. It was this relationship that led me to call him to work with me at Paul W. Davis Systems, Inc. as my personal assistant. It was one of the best business decisions I have ever made. He went anywhere and did anything I asked him to do and always did it well. He was the person who discovered that the State of Florida was starting a program that required that any person wanting to have a general contracting business would be required to pass a test proving they were qualified to do so. I did not want to take the test but he convinced me that it was necessary. He brought me what books were available for study, and then he stood in my stead concerning all business matters to allow me to study. The test day came and I found myself sitting in a group of about sixty contractors, most of whom did contracting work far over my head. A score of 70 was required to pass. I got a 72. Not good, but it served my purpose as well as a score of 100 would have. In retrospect, I can see that without that license, I would never have been able to expand the business and the ability to franchise would never have presented itself. Bill also opened and built the first branch office, which became our first franchise. I am forever grateful to Bill, a man who placed responsibility and Christian living above all else. He was truly my right arm.

Bill Horn

In the early stages of our expansion, Bill's cousin was our franchisee in West Palm Beach, Florida. Bill lived in Louisville, Kentucky, and called to express his interest in Paul W. Davis, Inc. I went to Louisville to meet with him and his wife Frankie. We talked for some time and Bill decided he wanted to buy the franchise rights to the Louisville area. He paid me one-half of the $20,000 franchise fee and agreed to bring the other half when he came to Florida for training. It was much later that I learned that the check was all the money they had other than Frankie's income as a school bus driver. Bill came a few weeks later for training, and he was on his way to becoming a very successful Paul W. Davis, Inc. franchisee. No other franchisee had the same positive impact that Bill Horn had on the total organization's success. He helped many other franchises become successful, in addition to being successful himself. In 1988, Bill relocated to Jacksonville to assume the presidency of the corporation for a brief period and then moved back to his true interest, which was and still is franchise ownership. He's keeping it in the family: his general manager is his son, Charlie Horn.

Mark Mullins

Mark was a man I met through my membership in a businessmen's group called The Executive Committee. We met once a month to listen to experts who spoke on managing and growing our individual businesses.

Mark had resigned his job as president of a very large company in the north. He came to Florida to form his own company that built and sold various types of work trailers. That market became overcrowded and he sold the business. I knew through our Executive Committee meetings that he was looking for a job and I knew that Paul Davis Systems was rapidly outgrowing my limited business experience. We agreed on a salary and the division of the workloads and Mark came to join me.

The change in the administration of the business was immediate. Mark and I did not always agree, but we never argued. He was too smart for that. His response to any suggestion I made that he did not feel would be good for the company was, "Paul, help me to understand." That put me in the position of having to prove the value of my suggestion. One of the dumbest things I did in my entire working life was to let Mark leave.

Gaylord Gerber

Gaylord was a tremendous help to me in the beginning years of the franchise program. I would tell Gaylord about some issue I faced in the business and without fail, he would tell me a solution and his solution always worked. So, in a short time I hired him. And even now, years later, I still have tremendous respect and great appreciation for him.

Dave Kelly

Dave was our marketing arm for the sale of new franchise territories. He also became the marketing arm for existing franchisees who wished to sell. Let me note here a fact that almost all small businesses face when it is time for them to exit the business they own: They can't sell to a competitor because they can't demonstrate the ability to transfer their clients to the purchaser. They can't sell to individuals looking to buy a business at a price that would fairly reward the seller. So most small business owners end up just selling their hard assets for a very small price. An example:

- The Tampa franchise, owned by Don Goldberg, was growing at a fast pace. The franchisee hired his uncle to become a sales/estimator/job manager.

- The uncle did well in estimating, sales and job management. He made a very good income based on a percentage of the sales, while adding value to the franchise operations.

- The time came when the uncle decided he could do without his nephew and, even though he had signed a two-year non-competition agreement, he left the company and started his own business, taking with him several of the company's best customers. The franchise owner did not want a family fight and therefore made no effort to enforce the non-compete clause.

- A few years later, the uncle decided to sell his business and retire. He spent a lot of time and effort seeking a buyer. No one was interested. Those who knew the business saw no value since they could get the business on their own when the existing business closed.

- Those prospects who did not know the business saw it as too complicated. At the end of the day, the uncle had no choice but to sell off his hard assets—which were few—and walk away. Don Goldberg, following the system we devised, increased his sales and profits and when he was ready to exit, not only received a fair price for his company, but guaranteed an income for himself and his wife for their lifetimes.

Clarence Steifel

Clarence was not an employee of the company; he was my life insurance agent. I met him when I was trying to be an insurance agent. His was a great success story and mine was a great failure story. His greatest single influence on my life occurred when he gave me a small Norman Vincent Peale booklet and urged me to read it. I placed it on a small table in my office, where it stayed for several weeks.

Back then there were two franchisees who continually created problems for me: one robbed me of the royalties on jobs he performed using our system, and the other often stirred up problems among the franchisees. One day I needed to get my mind off a number of negative issues so I picked up the booklet, moved to a comfortable chair, and read it end to end. It was a very helpful book. The part that struck me most was along the lines of: Forgive those who sin against you, in order that your sins will be forgiven and you can enjoy the peace of God, which passes all understanding.

I laid the book down, closed my eyes, and called to my mind two people in my organization who had and were continuing to betray my trust, and in so doing were creating a lot of anger, resentment and stress. They were both franchisees, a woman and a man. I brought the woman into my mind first, prayed and by faith I said, in my mind, "I forgive you." And I felt the anger and hurt disappear. I brought the man into my mind, thought about what he had done to me and in my mind, by faith, I prayed and said, "I forgive you." And I felt the anger and pain go away. For the first time in months I experienced the peace of God, was able to sleep without sleeping pills and could concentrate on the important tasks I faced each day.

I never told either of them that I had forgiven them. They probably would have thought I was crazy because neither of them thought cheating me was wrong. But they were out of my head and a new experience of God's peace began. One of the two left and the other continued to be a major factor as a leader in the franchise organization. With her I took the advice of Congressman Sam Rayburn of Texas, "Hug your friends, but hug your enemies even closer."

Good advice. My version is: Don't let your enemies live in your head.

Chapter 8
PAUL'S PEARLS, AND OTHER THOUGHTS OF NOTE

Anyway

In 1968, Kent M. Keith published a pamphlet titled "The Silent Revolution: Dynamic Leadership in the Student Council." In the booklet were "The Paradoxical Commandments of Leadership," a challenge of sorts for people to do what is right. Over the years, the ten points have been attributed to many people, most often to Mother Teresa, since they were posted on the wall of her children's home in Calcutta. Here they are in their original form:

1. People are illogical, unreasonable, and self-centered. Love them anyway.
2. If you do good, people will accuse you of selfish ulterior motives. Do good anyway.
3. If you are successful, you win false friends and true enemies. Succeed anyway.
4. The good you do today will be forgotten tomorrow. Do good anyway.
5. Honesty and frankness make you vulnerable. Be honest and frank anyway.
6. The biggest men with the biggest ideas can be shot down by the smallest men with the smallest minds. Think big anyway.
7. People favor underdogs, but follow only top dogs. Fight for a few underdogs anyway.

8. What you spend years building may be destroyed overnight. Build anyway.
9. People really need help but may attack you if you do help them. Help people anyway.
10. Give the world the best you have and you'll get kicked in the teeth. Give the world the best you have anyway.

This advice has stood me in good stead over the years. I urge you to copy it and place it where you can't help but see it from time to time.

Manage for Profit

It is not about doing things better. It's about doing things differently to obtain a better result.

It is not about working harder. It's about working by a system that guarantees a positive result.

It is not about managing people. It's about managing a program that guarantees your profit.

It is not about a system that ties you down. It's about a system that frees you up to expand your business to other areas with no investment and no risk.

It is not about exiting your business by shutting down. It's about a system that creates a resale value of an average of one-third of your annual sales.

It is not about reducing profits because of the insurer's choice of an estimating system or a "Contractor Connection"-type program. It's about sharing the fee and insuring your profit, regardless of the system.

It is not about a group of ideas. It's about a program built on one of Paul Davis's principles: Write stuff down.

The I's Have It

The same I's that started Paul Davis Systems on its way to success are the same I's that can give you an edge in your business.

Success in business is not a result of votes, but it is very much a result of rote. Rote is the use of memory, carried out without thought; the use of a system to attain a desired result.

The nine words I write about here will not in and of themselves make your business successful. It would be a fatal error to think so. But experience has taught me that they are essential if you are to differentiate your business from that of your competitors.

Integrity

Integrity is defined by Merriam-Webster as 1: firm adherence to a code of especially moral or artistic values; 2: an unimpaired condition. Every person or group of persons whose life your life touches deserves to benefit from your integrity. The major changes Paul Davis Systems introduced into the property insurance business were accepted by insurers because of our reputation of integrity.

It takes consistency to build a reputation of integrity. But it takes only one small deviation to destroy that trust. That might not sound fair, but it is a fact.

Inspiration

Inspiration is defined by Merriam-Webster as the act of inspiring; to infuse life, to influence, move or guide; to exhibit an inspired influence; to spur on.

Many of us have a tendency to excite our people, but excitement soon dies out. Inspiration is far more lasting. You can inspire your people by having a written, practical program to follow; by having pride in your company as a leader; by publicly praising staff for any job well done; by encouraging them to feel free to ask questions and offer suggestions.

One of the things that inspired me to do things differently was my fear of head-to-head competition. One of the lasting inspirations of my business life has been the old Rotary motto, "He profits most who serves the best."

Incentive

Incentives don't have to be trips to Vegas; you can work incentives into every day on the job:

- praise, properly delivered, also known as crediting
- reward for productivity, not for being present
- titles, which increase self-esteem
- the grant of authority to make decisions within the parameters of the system.

Inquisitive

Encouraging your people, and you, to stay inquisitive will keep the business thriving. You and your employees should always be:

- seeking knowledge, information and instructions
- willing to continue to learn
- asking themselves the question, "If there were no restrictions, what would I do?"
- looking for opportunities to make small changes or corrections.

Interested

Pay attention, even to small things.

Never let your mind wander when your customer is speaking, or anyone else is for that matter.

The more you can get your customer or prospect to talk, the more you will come to understand his or her business concerns and problems.

Care about your employees. They are the ones who can get you to where you want to go. Care about them as individuals, not as a group. Make sure you listen to their problems as though they are your problems. In the truest sense, they *are* your problems.

The following story, which still warms my heart every time I think of it, occurred while I still owned and operated the business. There was a lady who worked in Brenda's department and had done so for many years. She decided to retire and on her last Friday, Brenda and all her staff took her to lunch to say good-bye. On the following

Monday, she had a doctor's appointment. When it was over, she called Brenda in tears with the news that she had terminal cancer. Brenda came to my office to give me the news. It did not require rocket science to recognize that she was without income and also without health insurance.

We were both heartbroken for her. After some discussion, we decided the right thing to do was to put her back on our payroll for as long as she lived and that automatically reinstated her health insurance. She expressed her gratitude right up until her death some three months later. I still get a good feeling, even as I write this years later.

Interacting Opportunities

Look for opportunities to provide value for your customer that require a commitment on their part to obtain that value. Expecting a prospective customer to change vendors just because you are a nice guy is a pipe dream. Focus on added-value opportunities.

Innovation, the Ultimate "I"

Trying to do things better than others in your business is a hard row to hoe. And it is hard for your prospect to see your company as a better way to go.

Innovation is the introduction of something new or very different from the current norm in your business field that adds value to the operations and profitability of your customers. Innovation often leads to more innovation. And as long as the innovation adds value to your customer's business, the more the better.

Remember: "All change is stressful, even good change."

Before you introduce change, ask yourself the following questions:
- Will it affect our customers' or clients' business in a positive manner?
- Will it have a positive or a negative effect on our current operations?
- Will it have a positive effect on company profits?

Information

Information is power. Before you sit down with your customer or prospect, be sure you have done your due diligence on their company. When you're sitting in their office your objective is to get clarity on one or more of their operations to which you want to add value.

Years back, Mark Mullins taught me how to ask a question without causing offense. When we would disagree on an issue, he would always put me on the spot with the request, "help me to understand." I guarantee you that it is an effective way to get information without offending.

In-sourcing

When you out-source a product or task, the advantage is that you know that the product or task will be delivered or performed for a preset price. In-sourcing allows you to accomplish the same goal using your own in-house people.

In-sourcing requires:
- a clear understanding of the task to be performed and the result to be achieved
- a formal contract between the parties
- a fixed formula for compensation to the service provider based on a percentage of the selling price of the finished product or service
- an agreement as to how and when the compensation will be paid
- agreement by the service provider that he or she will honor the value system and culture of the business
- a two-year written contract in which the service providers agree not to reveal any trade secrets and not to compete in the particular field for two years after either party terminates the agreement.

Ready, Fire, Aim

Long before Tom Peters, the business guru, made the ready-fire-aim concept popular as a modern-day business principle, I was using it to build Paul W. Davis Systems, Inc. I therefore feel qualified to address the issue from a personal perspective. In my case, ready, fire, aim was not driven by any special marketing service, production or business strategy. It was, simply put, the only way I knew how to build a business.

If you don't know how to accomplish a particular goal, it seems obvious that you start as best you know how, in the general direction you wish to go, and correct your aim as you move toward that mark.

My brother Charles and I served as 20-mm-gun loaders on Liberty ships as part of our service in WWII. Navy gunners were taught to track and hit the target by ready, fire, aim. Ready consisted of the gunner donning his helmet and strapping himself into the gun harness, as the loader took a magazine of shells from the ammunition box and snapped it onto the gun. The gunner cocked his weapon, faced the target and started firing. He had valuable assets: a fully loaded cannon capable of delivering death and destruction to the enemy, specific knowledge of where the enemy was and the direction in which the enemy was moving. This was enough information in the pre-computer, pre-radar-aimed weapons of today to begin the process, but not sufficient to take accurate aim.

The process was designed to be ready, fire, aim because the gunner was enabled to aim through the act of firing. Every third shell in the magazine was a tracer: a shell that burned phosphorus stored in the rear of the projectile. This allowed the gunner to see where his projectiles were going and by moving the bright line created by the tracers he could move those projectiles up, down, forward or back to the place where they and the target met.

In order to accept the ready-fire-aim principle in business, you must have the confidence to know that you have plenty of bullets (some will surely miss the mark), and that you have a clear enough understanding of your objective that you can track and measure your actions and continually correct your aim.

It is interesting to note here that as a business seeks to serve its customers, those customers' needs are continually changing. We must be quick to change our aim by tracking that change if we are to be successful in delivering the then-needed product or services where our customers will be when the delivery arrives.

Given the ever-increasing rate of change in the business environment, it seemed only logical to me that ready, aim, fire should be the norm, with its opportunity to design and perfect a service or product prior to the beginning of the delivery process.

My dependence on a ready-fire-aim approach was increased by my commitment to differentiate our business operation from that of the competition. To carry that dependence to a higher level, many of the programs initiated by the company were programs never attempted before.

It isn't the purpose here to give you the impression that we did not strive for excellence, but I did not feel that perfectionism was a logical platform from which to grow a successful business. Perfectionist tendencies create unrealistic expectations, tremendous stress, and an inability to appreciate who you are and to look at yourself with kind eyes.

A speaker at our office made the following statement: "It is all right to strive for perfection. You will never reach perfection, but you may discover excellence along the way." This seemed to be a very logical and practical approach to perfectionism. Not all who try to perfect a service or product before they expose it to the marketplace are perfectionists. Most are just people who want to deliver excellence. This is very commendable but still creates a goal for which success is improbable.

The best judge as to the accuracy of your aim is the end user. It is okay to provide an imperfect service or product so long as it meets a few simple requirements: your service or product is better than what is on the market at the time; you are willing to continually correct your aim for the service or product; you are willing to make good for any customer who suffers as a result of those imperfections.

Given you can accept those requirements, ready, fire, aim becomes a learning process. You learn what your customers want. You will learn how to create and implement processes. You may never be known for reaching perfection, but you will be perceived as an innovator who is constantly seeking ways to help your customers.

Starting with less than perfection means you may fail, but if success is simply the process of failing forward, it is imperative that each of us has the right to try and fail as often as is necessary. Ready, fire, aim guarantees that at least you will start. Waiting to perfect your service or product may mean you will never start. Herein lies a great truth: not everything you start will succeed, but nothing you don't start can succeed.

The lesson here is not that you should look for ways to implement ready, fire, aim in everything you undertake. The lesson is, if you have a good idea, don't be afraid to develop it as well as you reasonably can, and start firing. You will be amazed at how well you can correct your aim if you're willing to simply track and measure your efforts.

Sand Dollars: A Vintage Speech

If there is something I enjoy almost more than putting my thoughts on paper, it's sharing my thoughts with others. I particularly love speaking at company gatherings, to the bright young recruits and to our experienced franchisees alike. This is a speech I made at a Paul Davis convention in Birmingham, Alabama.

For several years, my younger children, Emily and Paul Jr., and I spent the week between Christmas and New Year's at The Cloister on Sea Island, Georgia.

One of our favorite pastimes was walking the beaches at low tide looking for sand dollars, a beautifully shaped shell that bleaches out white with five oblong holes all the way through the shell and the outline of a five-pointed star on the top.

If you can walk, if you can see, if you can bend or stoop and if your arms and hands work properly, it is a very easy job to locate and pick up sand dollars on top of the sand. All you need to know is what they look like, that they can only be found at the beach and that it is best to look for them at low tide. This is not a very complicated task. The only problem is that with so many people doing the same thing, you very seldom find sand dollars that way.

One day, after many years of looking for and finding sand dollars on the sand, competing with my beach-walking, surface-searching peer group, I made a discovery that led me to a dramatic increase in the number of sand dollars the kids and I could find.

What I saw in the sand was a slightly irregular, half-round outline that could be seen only because the sand of the outline was raised just a fraction of an inch. When I bent over and slipped my fingers under this raised edge, there, buried beneath the surface of the sand was a completely whole sand dollar. The outline was a result of the sand dollar working its way under the wet sand and settling in at a slightly canted angle.

Now, I had discovered a technique of searching for sand dollars that allowed me to find sand dollars under the surface of the sand where only a few of my beach-walking peer group could find them.

Having discovered this new technique, I found myself enjoying these beach searches even more and soon began to look for other telltale signs of sand dollars hidden beneath the surface. One day I noticed three oblong-shaped indentations in the sand that were spread in a quarter-circle pattern. The spacing was similar to the spacing of the three larger holes in the sand dollar. Lights flashed, bells rang and I bent and slipped my fingers around the edge of this pattern on the sand, and, lo and behold, another beautiful sand dollar.

Now I had a second technique for searching, and the number of those of my beach-walking peer group who could find as many sand dollars as I could became even less, while my success and enjoyment of the task increased tremendously.

Then as I walked the beach, I found myself always looking for more telltale signs, trying to find another searching technique to add to my success and consequential enjoyment of searching for and finding sand dollars. I found one or two additional small clues and each one brought me to a higher level of success and even closer to the top of my beach-walking peer group.

Perhaps there is an important lesson here about life in general. Those of us who tend to skim the surface of life can never see nor find what is hidden from plain view, and tend to win very few of the prizes life holds in store for those who constantly hone their people skills and God-given talents.

On one trip, the kids and I were walking and the beach was pretty crowded. Right to our left was a man and his son who was probably five or six years old. He saw us finding sand dollars when, with all the surface shells picked over, he was finding none. Finally, I spoke to him and asked if he was having any luck. He said, "You know, my son wants to find a sand dollar so badly, but we can't find one. Could you help?" We took a few minutes to show him what we were looking for and then his son was ecstatic when he found not one but several sand dollars.

Isn't it great that although we all have to learn by experience, the experience does not always have to be our own.

A "know it all" will not learn. A self-satisfied individual will not seek new knowledge, and yet here was someone with such a great desire to succeed in this small endeavor that he was willing to learn from our experiences.

Learning successful techniques is one of the great secrets of success.

Many times, as I think of the franchise organization and the greatly differing measures of success enjoyed by members of this peer group, I am reminded of my experiences with sand dollars.

There is so much insurance restoration business available that it really only takes a few very basic skills to get a share of the jobs.

If you don't believe that this is so, look at some of your competitors. As I think back about some of mine, I am amazed that they could survive in our business, but many of them did and still do. People who have no more basic skills in sales or management or business than the average beach-walking searcher has in locating sand dollars, yet they survive.

If you walk along the beach long enough, you will find some sand dollars. If you talk to enough adjusters and agents, you'll get some insurance restoration jobs. Enough to survive, and that's a pretty simple job.

My problem has always been that although I am proud to consider myself a survivor, surviving is not my primary goal. I always strive for success. I don't want to be just one of my peer group. I want to be the leader of my peer group. I don't just want to hold on to my business, I want to see it grow and expand. My goal is not to earn $100,000 a year; it is to earn $200,000 a year, then $300,000, then more. The difference between survival and success is the difference between night and day.

As you look at our peer group, the entire franchise organization, it is easy to distinguish the successes from the survivors. By successes I mean sales and profits. For the first without the second is meaningless. The success stories are not always the hardest workers, nor the best educated, nor the best financed. Neither do they have the best territories, nor the greatest luck, or some unique set of circumstances that have assured their success.

The true difference between the successes and the survivors is that although the successful franchisees do not always work harder, they do always work smarter. In the past, they have developed certain techniques for success in the insurance restoration contracting business, and they almost without exception continue to search for and develop new techniques to make them even more successful.

Think about the logic of this. It applies to every area of life. I love tennis and I have often said that the only things lacking in my game are quickness, agility and technique. The only one I can do anything about, the one that will do me the greatest good, is technique.

We tend to think of technique only in terms of the sciences, the professions, perhaps sport and almost assuredly, only in relation to other people and other situations. That is so sad because the primary difference between working hard and working smart is the discovery and mastery of techniques that apply to our particular business endeavor.

Each of you can discover and develop the necessary techniques to make you more successful in the insurance restoration contracting business. If you're willing to devote the time and effort, it is not all that difficult.

In the old Amos and Andy program on radio, Amos once asked the King Fish why he had such good judgment. "Well," said the King Fish, "good judgment comes from experience." "Then where does experience come from?" asked Amos. "From bad judgment," answered the King Fish.

You learn by your mistakes. Your objective is that you not make the same mistake twice. You think back to see what you did wrong and then you plan how to not make the same mistake again by remembering this and putting it to work the next time that situation arises. You develop a technique for eliminating that particular problem.

You also learn by your successes. Your objective is to repeat those things that did work well for you and improve on them. You think back about what you did that was good. And about what could be improved, and then you plan how to make this work even better. By remembering this and putting it to work the next time that situation arises you develop a technique to gain success in that particular situation.

See how simple it is? Can you imagine how much you will learn from this process? Can you picture in your mind what successes this will bring you ten, fifteen, twenty years from now? Most of us truly cannot conceive of how successful we might be if we did this for twenty years. This is the way most people in small businesses learn techniques. It is a long, drawn-out process that pays big dividends in the end.

Wouldn't it be great if all those years of learning could be condensed to a matter of months, so that we can begin to enjoy the fruits of that learning by a greater experience of success right now?

How fantastic it would be if someone could come along with eight or ten tried and proven techniques that we could learn and master in a matter of weeks rather than years.

It would be even more amazing if these successful techniques had been developed for the insurance restoration contracting business and could be applied directly to our own business, in our own city, each and every day beginning right now.

What would it be worth to you if you could purchase a book that contained particular techniques to meet and solve almost every problem you face in operating your business? With each technique having been proven to be successful time after time over a period of twenty years?

The icing on the cake would be to be a friend of the author of this book, the very person who had either developed or been involved in the development and testing of each of these proven techniques. To be able to discuss these techniques personally with this author whenever you need clarification of a particular point or lack some understanding of how to apply the lessons learned from that book.

Would you believe that all of these techniques are already in a book that is sitting somewhere in your office at this very moment? That you cannot only discover the techniques in that book, but that you can learn how to implement and master each one in a very short period of time.

The book is the *Paul Davis Systems Operations Manual* and it is chockfull of sales and management techniques to make your life much easier, to allow you to work much smarter, and work fewer hours, and to make your business more successful than you have ever dreamed was possible.

Let me share an idea that can transform your business. Have a motivational meeting once a month. I don't want to call it a sales meeting because you have tried that and all you talk about are problems, bad subcontractors, crazy property owners and uncollected jobs. Everyone goes away thoroughly dejected and defeated.

I want you to have an old-fashioned, positive, upbeat meeting. Don't talk about problems, talk about successes. Be happy about how far you have come. Praise everyone who has done anything well. Express appreciation for your staff. Talk about their potential. Get excited about your goals and fill the air with goodwill. Allow time for food and fellowship before the meeting—it does not need to be expensive. Pizza and beer at the office is fine if that suits your belief system. Get a good family spirit going, and keep it that way.

Each month, choose one of the techniques found in the operations manual to highlight. Spend at least thirty minutes discussing that one technique and deciding how it can best be implemented in your business. Try this upbeat meeting once a month for three months and I guarantee you the results will be dramatic. Remember, no problems, no complaints—just praise, appreciation and enthusiasm.

If you are alone in your franchise, you can do one of two things: find someone within driving distance and join them each month, or, if that is impossible, work alone by devoting fifteen minutes each morning to reading through the operations manual. Don't try for speed; try for comprehension, and make a special effort to apply and master at least one technique each week.

Remember, success is a growth process. We grow by learning and applying that knowledge. It only takes desire and will. Role models are vital to success and we have some excellent role models in our company. But remember, role models are only vital in relation to their successes.

There is not a person who has made more mistakes than I have, and if you want to emulate those mistakes, you can, with very little effort, fail. Although I have made many mistakes, I have also learned from those mistakes and developed techniques to try to prevent them from happening again. Because of this, I can say with absolute truth that not too many people in this room have experienced more success than I have. A good rule to follow is, never emulate a person's failures; learn from them. Emulate a person's successful techniques and you will profit from them.

The greatest difference between being successful and failing is that our successful business owners work not harder, but smarter. The difference between working hard and working smart is the discovery and mastery of successful techniques for operating your insurance restoration contracting business. Anyone can scratch the surface and survive. But with a little more effort, a little more digging, you can learn to find the real treasure of your own business success.

Good techniques work. If you are diligent in your search for sand dollars, you will find sand dollars. If you are diligent in your search for success, you will find success. Make your pledge today: I can and I will master the techniques required and they will make me successful!

Poetry

One might think that for a person who took English 10B for three semesters writing would be anathema. Not so. Writing is a pleasure for me, whether it's building systems, creating speeches, figuring out operations manuals, but my favorite has to be poetry. I'm including three poems here, one from earlier days, and two written for the love of my life.

Clean Out of Debt

At 7 a.m. I kiss my honey,
Taking coffee out the door,
Working two jobs 'cause I need the money.
Everybody's always asking for more.

I owe for last year's great vacations.
I owe for last year's Christmas toys.
I owe for two birthday celebrations.
Not to mention last week's joys.

Borrowed to buy a dress for my honey.
Borrowed to buy me a new Corvette.
Lord, if I could just borrow enough money,
I know I could get clean out of debt.

Got a fantastic buy on a new TV,
Saved a thousand bucks on a brand new car.
Bought three suits and got one free.
There's bargains man, wherever you are.

Found a neat time-share down the strand.
Signed to completely refurnish and decorate.
Bought a payment calendar to know where I stand.
I've got thirty-nine payments, and every one late.

Got so many bills it's ceased to be funny.
Gonna see my banker, I'm tired of this sweat.
Lord, if he will just lend me the money,
I think I'll finally be clean out of debt.

Our First Year

It happened last year on December ten,
We each took our lover, our dearest friend,
To have and to hold, to share in each life,
And you, my Sweet Brenda, became my dear wife.

This year has been busy, with our hectic pace,
Of goings and comings and finding our place,
We've lived on the edge in a dizzying whirl,
But someway, somehow we've covered our world.

We've mended some fences long fallen down,
And reached out together to folks all around,
We've established a oneness for others to see
And in all that is done, it is now you and me.

We've started a family in this our first year,
Creating a bond between those we hold dear,
By investing our time, our love and our giving,
We set them example of sharing and living.

We've worked in our business and seen it grow stronger,
And set some new goals to grow it still longer,
We've talked and consulted and energized one another,
And in the doing found, we work well with each other.

So much has gone on in the outer edges,
Through input and output, commitments and pledges,
But the part with most meaning, the part that is true,
Is the part of just sharing my whole life with you.

We two are now one, in the real sense that's true
But I think even more we each are now two.
We do share each other's mind, body and soul
But we still each exist in our particular mold.

You live in my heart and dwell in my mind,
Your influence is there, your presence so kind
So that each action I take and each thing I do
Flows freely from me and expresses you.

I live in your being and dwell in your soul,
My presence and love touch all you control
So every place that you go and every person you see,
And everything that you touch is touched by me.

For two to be one is a marvelous feat,
But for each to be two, is a more special treat,
Reserved only for those whose love is so giving
The whole heart's desire is the other's rich living.

And now to the close of this year of beginning,
How fast it has gone, how quickly it's ending,
It was filled with emotion of all shapes and sizes,
We found what we sought but we still found surprises.

And now for the highlight of this year we shared.
The first of the many we'll have 'cause we dared,
To step out together, to overcome great fear,
To create this union which we now hold so dear.

The highlight of highlights among many indeed,
Is that without exception, you've met my need,
And with all your influence the one thing I find,
That in every situation you're gentle with my mind.

So I love you sweet Brenda even more now than then,
You're not only my lover, but truly my best friend,
I treasure our marriage and you as my wife,
And treasure the sharing with you, of my life.

Happy Birthday
My Sweet Brenda

How many times have I done this before,
For the only woman I truly adore?
While most of the married men I know,
Go out to find gifts, their love to show.

I know the quote "actions louder than words,"
But it's easier to buy, than to create the words.
And at the end of the day, of what we say and do,
Only words can describe my great love for you.

When I think about where we are today,
And I try to remember how we got this way.
What amazed me in the beginning, still amazes me today,
And my prayer is that God will keep it this way.

We are told about life, it can't last forever
And the saying is true, but not really clever.
It's an obvious fact, we both know is true.
But as long as I draw breath, I will still love you.

Paul
3-11-12

EPILOGUE

Paul Woodall Davis started his insurance restoration contracting company with a focus on the Golden Rule–Do unto others as you would have them do unto you–and the original Rotary motto "He profits most who serves best" as a guiding principle. By valuing home-owners, insurers and subcontractors, and continually improving on processes, the company has grown from start-up financing of $2,500 to approaching $1B in North American sales this year.

Since Paul sold his company in 1997, Paul Davis has stayed the course, continuing as an innovator and premier provider of disaster mitigation and restoration services. In a similar fashion, the innovations have been shared, built upon and as a result many more companies have sprung from PDRI. Steady progressive growth is one measure of success for Paul Davis, but just as important is the fact that Paul Davis franchisees are some of the largest and most respected restoration specialists in the industry.

In 2000, the company name was changed to Paul Davis Restoration, Inc. in the U.S.; the Paul Davis Restoration franchise count then was 217. In 2003, PDRI began exploring newer and less invasive drying technologies that could reduce the drying time for a water-damaged home from six to eight days down to just three to four days. This was a cutting-edge, game-changing concept that was not adopted by the industry for another eight to ten years. In mid-decade we adopted the Net Promoter Score from The Ultimate Question; we were the first in the industry to adopt the system. Just as Paul Davis was first to develop computerized estimating and job-costing systems, again PDRI was leading the pack.

Training started out as pulling up a chair at Paul's desk back in the early seventies. In 2005, PDRI built one of the nation's very few structural flood houses and training centers. By 2010, the National Training Centre had grown to a 17,000-square-foot facility with a full-scale 1,700-square-foot house inside. The fully furnished house has a living room, kitchen, bathroom and bedroom, and is regularly flooded with thousands of gallons of water so trainees get hands-on experience at techniques like the revolutionary Dry-in-3, another innovation by the company. Other training modules include fire, smoke, inspecting, valuing, cleaning and restoring. In 2008, Paul Davis helped develop on-site technology called MICA (Mobile Information Collaborative Application) to record and document the drying of a structure to monitor, demonstrate and prove the effectiveness of the drying process to the property owner and the insurance company. A contents processing facility and trauma/bio-hazard training mock-ups were added to the training center in 2014.

Paul Davis Emergency Services (PDES) started in the U.S. in 2009; seven franchises were sold in the first year; in 2010, the PDES count was 30 franchises. The year 2014 saw the merging of the American and Canadian Paul Davis companies when FirstService Brands acquired Paul Davis Systems Canada. The move added 63 franchises to Paul Davis Restoration and unified the PD brand across North America under one leadership team. By 2015, the number of Paul Davis Emergency Services franchises rose to 114, and there were 257 Paul Davis Restoration franchises, for a total of 371 PD franchises.

The more things change, the more they stay the same, and that is true in the insurance restoration business. Insurance carriers are focusing on providing service to their clients, as is Paul Davis. As repairs and restoration have become more and more technically advanced and engineered, what remains is the ability to create a meaningful and "restorative" experience that creates relief for the homeowners in their time of need. Given the values that Paul used to start the business and the legacy that remains, PD's Golden Rule makes PDR uniquely positioned to continue to grow in the market and adapt to client needs.

The future will also include an increased use of environmentally neutral processes and products in the mitigation and restoration of damaged property. Already ahead in that category with the creation of the Drying in Place process that saves time, gas and energy in restoring a water loss, PDR will continue the journey into the future relying on environmentally friendly products and processes.

Fifty years is a landmark anniversary, and one we all take great pride in celebrating. Thank you to all our franchisees, staff members, insurers, homeowner clients and friends, subcontractors and tradespeople, suppliers and vendors, and welcome to those people who will join us for the next fifty years.

TIMELINE 1966-1997

1966

- Dissolution of Golden Crown Builders, Inc.
- Paul starts Paul W. Davis Contracting, a one-man insurance restoration contracting business with start-up capital of $2,500
- Jean Nicholson, from Golden Crown, joins Paul
- After the first eight months of operation sales reach $200,000

1967

- On January 17, Paul incorporates as Paul W. Davis, Inc. and then changes the name to Paul W. Davis Systems, Inc., a Florida Corporation
- Paul's brother Charles Davis joins in marketing
- The office moves from a corner of a warehouse to a garage apartment

1968

- Bill Richardson joins the office as assistant to the president
- PDS builds and opens the new office behind the old office, where the company remains until 1984
- First branch office opens in Orlando. A new corporation is formed called Paul W. Davis Systems of Orlando

1969

- Paul writes the first Paul Davis Systems Operations Manual
- The idea of franchising the unique operating system Paul had developed in the three years since 1966 is explored and set in motion
- Paul's brother Bill Davis expresses interest in converting the Orlando corporation branch office into a PDS franchise

1970

- On January 17 Don Goldberg becomes the first franchise owner of PDS of Tampa, with financial partner Dr. Edgar Cooper
- In January controlling interest in the Orlando corporation changes hands and it becomes the second franchise
- Paul incorporates Paul W. Davis International Corp. This is also a Florida Corporation that has the exclusive rights to establish franchise operations in other countries
- By year's end there are five franchises, all in Florida, plus the original Jacksonville operation

1971

- Continued growth of the franchise operations
- First serious attempt at aggressive expansion
- Harry Elrod joins as sales manager for franchising
- More top-level staff members are added

1972

- By year's end the debt load requires scaling back on expansion plans and cutting head office staff back to Paul and two others
- Paul's wife is facing critical illness
- Paul sells the Jacksonville franchise. It goes through three owners in the next six years

1973
- Continued financial problems at PDS
- Paul's wife dies
- Paul restructures the existing franchise relationships and retires at age 46

1978
- The third owner of the Jacksonville franchise is having problems; asks Paul to take over temporarily in October. He never tries to regain control.
- Sarasota is the first franchise to exceed $1M in sales in a calendar year

1979
- Local franchise thriving
- Sales growing
- Franchises have dropped from 19 to 13 due to lack of direction. Paul starts slowly adding units as he takes the leadership role

1980
- Great local growth
- Some increase in the system
- Jean Nicholson returns to assist in growth of restoration business

1981
- Chip Lofton joins to expand the franchise organization
- Decision is made to computerize the Paul Davis operating system; money raised by selling the rights to use the then-undeveloped system to several of the existing franchises

1982

- Computerized estimating system is completed; program positions PDS as leader in the industry
- Work on job cost accounting system is started
- Franchise system growing slowly
- Local restoration business continues to expand rapidly to become the largest in the system

1983

- In June, Paul sells the local restoration business and it becomes a local franchise
- In September, Paul leases the St. Augustine Road office and moves to an office on Cesery Boulevard with staff to build an international franchise system
- 19 franchises

1984

- Increased growth in franchise system
- Building of business plan
- Formed first truly independent board of directors in a move toward structure and accountability. Paul feels this to be one of the most meaningful events in his business life

1985

- Disastrous council meeting in Hilton Head; betrayal from a trusted colleague. Paul suffers from exhaustion
- 45 franchises

1986

- PWD International grants master franchise rights to Bill Robinson for certain Canadian provinces; Paul retains rights to marks in Canada

- Bill Robinson is the first franchisee in Canada
- New council structure is accepted; franchisees become a self-governing body, sharing authority with the franchisor
- Completion Services Inc. was formed
- National sales program started

1987
- The security fund program is approved
- Council adopts the arbitration program

1988
- Bill Horn relocates to Jacksonville to assume presidency for a brief period
- The company needs even more space and moves to new offices at 8933 Western Way
- System grows in number and sales volume
- Paul begins to concentrate on development of management systems to better control fast-growing franchises
- Western provinces added to Bill Robinson's Canadian master franchise rights

1989
- Signature Professional Cleaning is started with Fred Thompson as director as an add-on franchise to existing PDS offices with the objective to get the franchises into the mitigation and cleaning portion of restoration work. Prior to this, Paul Davis franchises were generally reconstruction only and subcontracted emergency services. This was really the beginning of the full service contractor model the Paul Davis franchises have become
- Brenda Staver joins the company, and becomes Paul's wife

1990

- Mark Mullins takes control of operations as president and COO
- Paul moves to CEO
- Implementation of the Regional Marketing Director Program and positioning of six regional directors

1991

- Silver anniversary: 25 years
- 165 franchises across U.S. and Canada
- 28 employees from the original three
- Quebec added to Bill Robinson's Canadian master franchise rights
- Computer systems and operations manuals translated to French; Canadian Quebec franchises operate as "Les System Paul Davis"
- New thrust toward team building with insurers
- A new program of commitment to excellence has the theme "Learning from our past, transforming our present, committing to our future," developed by Brenda Davis

1992

- Fred Thompson dreams up ITEL, and starts testing carpet samples; ITEL soon becomes a division of Paul Davis. It is later sold to Mark Mullins when he leaves the position of president

1993

- New corporate headquarters and training center has more than 21,500 square feet adjacent to Baymeadows Country Club
- Paul Davis creates a laboratory for ITEL to test and determine the value of building materials to help insurance companies properly settle claims. This concept has saved insurance companies millions of dollars in overpayments due to improper valuation of building materials and finishes.

1994

- 1994 or 1995, at the request of USAA Insurance Company Paul designs Contractor Network Consultants (ultimately Contractor Connection) but was prevented from implementing it by a small group of franchisees

1995

- Scott Baker becomes president and CEO of Paul W. Davis Systems, Inc.

1997

- With 240 franchises, parent company Paul W. Davis Systems, Inc. (U.S. only) is sold to FirstService Corporation, a Canadian public company. Paul retains ownership of international operations in Canada, U.K. and Australia.

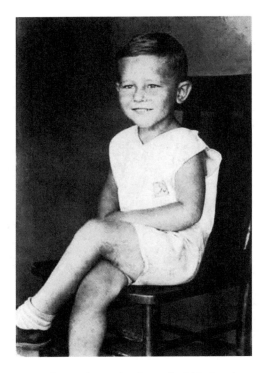

*Paul, age 3, in what he called his P-suit
because it had his initial on it, January 1930*

Paul before he received his PFC stripes, age 18,
when he was stationed at Fort Jackson, Virginia

All five of the boys in the backyard;
from left: Joe, Bob, Charlie, Bill and Paul, 1952

Paul's father and mother, Charles C. Davis, Sr.
and Mary Susan Woodall Davis, Florida, 1961

The very first office of Paul W. Davis Contracting—a 480-square-foot, second-floor office—at 3515 St. Augustine Road, Jacksonville, Florida, 1967. When the new office was move-in ready, Paul paid $1,000 to have this building demolished. Only after selling it did he discover the building was actually being moved down the street and sold to put $3,000 profit in someone else's pocket. Paul considers this house flip to be an early lesson to improve his management skills, but he always enjoys the telling of the story

The second office of Paul W. Davis Contracting, built by Paul and friends, behind the old office on St. Augustine Road

In keeping with Paul's desire to set his insurance restoration contacting business apart from any competitors, there was not a truck to be seen at the new Paul W. Davis Contracting office

Paul at his desk, late 1960s. This is typically what Paul's desk looks like even today, supporting the theory that a messy desk means a creative mind

Back in the day, new franchise owners pulled up a chair to Paul's desk for training. He still has the pipe-stand. Note his mug, "I love my Dad"

Paul cut a different figure in insurance restoration contracting, wearing a dress shirt, tie, jacket and properly pressed trousers when in the field for business. But no matter what the damage, he always wore a construction helmet to go in and scope the loss, 1970s

A franchise council meeting marking 15 years of franchising, 50 locations in 10 states, and over $68,000,000 in sales. The small print on the sign says, "With ever increasing quality and service, with continuous record-breaking sales and network expansion, we say, 'We're Just Beginning'"

Paul Davis honors the top sales associates at an awards ceremony; from left: Ted Porter, Bill Corley, Paul, Bill Horn, Chris Wiggins and Mike Waddell

124

Brenda's family at their wedding, Ponte Vedra, 1989

Paul's family at their wedding, Ponte Vedra, 1989

Brenda and Paul on their Hawaiian honeymoon cruise, 1990

A training class of new franchisees,
outside the Paul Davis building, 1990

Ed Austin, mayor of Jacksonville, congratulating Paul at a celebration of Jacksonville business owners, 1990

Paul and his brother Charlie at an open house for the new office building, complete with outdoor party tents, 1992

*Prospective Paul Davis franchisees from London, England,
interested in bringing PDS to the U.K. They brought their flag,
which was then hung in the office lobby*

The Jacksonville Times-Union *took this photo to illustrate a story about*
Paul W. Davis Systems, Inc. *Bill Robinson, the first Canadian franchisee
and master franchisor for Canada, is pictured seated.*

Paul in his retirement working in the yard, clearing trees, using the cart sent to him by Don Goldberg, the first PDS franchisee, as a retirement gift. Says Paul of this time, "We bought a nice home in Yulee. It was on about three and a half acres, a good part of which was wooded and overgrown with bushes and vines. One of my tasks—and a source of enjoyment for me—was to drive our tractor mower to keep the growth under control. One day as I was driving out of a grown-over area I suddenly realized that I was being attacked by bees whose ground hive I must have destroyed with the tractor. I was being stung over and over and started to run, but suddenly realized that I had left the tractor motor running. I ran back to the tractor, stopped the motor and started back for the house, bees still attacking. Our son Corey took me to the hospital where the nurse did what she could to help ease the pain of over one hundred and ten bee stings. This time, I really was dumb and ugly!"

*Paul's daughter Susan, with her children
Mark (front), Matthew, and Mary Beth, 1998*

*Mum, Dad and all the kids, or, the Davis-Staver Brady Bunch; from left,
standing: Mike, Rich, Emily, Corey, Paul Jr.; from left, seated: Debbie,
Brenda, Paul, Susan; at the house in Fernandina Beach, Florida, 2001*

Paul's daughter Emily, husband, Russ, and their son, Joshua

Paul and his granddaughter Mary Beth

Paul's son Paul Jr., his wife, Carley, with daughters Zoe (left) and Kia

Brenda's son Mike and his wife, Laura

Brenda's youngest son, Rich, and his wife, Mary Kay, with their children Brooke (seated), Lauren and Parker, 2009

Paul's oldest daughter, Debbie, and her daughter, Anisa

Brenda's son Corey, his wife, Kelly, and their children, from left, Cailey, Christian and Savannah

Brenda and Paul, 2010

Paul, photographed by the Jacksonville Business Journal for an article, 2010. Paul says jokingly, the photo is like him, always in the dark

Brenda and Paul celebrate with grandson Matthew,
home from the army for Christmas